# SPORT FOR LIFE

| | |
|---|---|
| **BOWLING** | Joyce M. Harrison<br>*Brigham Young University*<br>Ron Maxey |
| **CYCLING** | Lee N. Burkett<br>Paul W. Darst<br>*Arizona State University* |
| **JOGGING** | David E. Corbin<br>*The University of Nebraska at Omaha* |
| **RACQUETBALL** | Robert P. Pangrazi<br>*Arizona State University* |
| **STRENGTH TRAINING**<br>*Beginners, Bodybuilders, and Athletes* | Philip E. Allsen<br>*Brigham Young University* |

Charles B. Corbin/Philip E. Allsen, Series Editors

*SPORT FOR LIFE*

# BOWLING

**Joyce M. Harrison**
*Brigham Young University*

**Ron Maxey**

Charles B. Corbin/Philip E. Allsen, Series Editors

**Scott, Foresman and Company**
Glenview, Illinois         London

Cover photograph by Robert Drea

**Library of Congress Cataloging-in-Publication Data**

Harrison, Joyce M.
 Bowling.

 (Sport for life series)
 Includes index.
 1. Bowling. 2. Bowling—United States.
I. Maxey, Ron. II. Title. III. Series.
GV903.H37 1987    794.6      86-17753

ISBN 0-673-18324-6

Copyright © 1987
Scott, Foresman and Company.
All Rights Reserved.
Printed in the United States of America.

1 2 3 4 5 6 7 – MVN – 91 90 89 88 87 86

# Foreword

We are calling this series SPORT FOR LIFE because we believe a sports skills series should be more than just a presentation of the "rules of the game." A popular sport or activity should be presented in a way that encourages understanding through direct experience, improvement through prompt correction, and enjoyment through proper mental attitude.

Over the years, each SPORT FOR LIFE author has instructed thousands of people in their selected activity. We are delighted these "master teachers" have agreed to put down in writing the concepts and procedures they have developed successfully in teaching a skill.

The books in the SPORT FOR LIFE Series present other unique features as appropriate to the featured sport or activity.

**The Sport Experience:** This is a learning activity that explains and teaches a technique or specific rule. Whether it requires the reader to experience selecting a specific bicycle, stroking a backhand in tennis, or choosing an approach to use in bowling it carries the learner right to the heart of the game or activity at a pace matching his or her own progress. The Sport Experience is identified throughout the book with its own special typographical design.

**The Error Corrector:** The SPORT FOR LIFE authors have taken specific skills and listed some of the common errors encountered by participants; at the same time they have listed the methods to be utilized to correct these errors. The Error Corrector can be compared to a road map as it provides checkpoints toward skillful performance of a sport or activity.

**The Mental Game:** Understanding the mental game can remove many of the obstacles to success. The authors have devised techniques to aid the reader in planning playing strategy and in learning how to cope with the stress of competition. It is just as important to know how to remove mental errors as it is to deal with the physical ones.

The editors and authors of SPORT FOR LIFE trust that their approach and enthusiasm will have a lasting effect on each reader and will help promote a lifetime of health and happiness, physically and psychologically, for a sport well played or an activity well performed.

Charles B. Corbin/Philip E. Allsen

# About the Authors and Editors

***Joyce M. Harrison and Ron Maxey.*** Dr. Harrison is Professor of Physical Education and Coordinator of Undergraduate Professional Programs at Brigham Young University in Provo, Utah. She has authored numerous texts, articles, and films and is a member of many professional organizations, including the American Alliance of Health, Physical Education, Recreation and Dance. Mr. Maxey is a former instructor of physical education at Brigham Young University.

***Charles B. Corbin.*** Dr. Corbin is Professor of Physical Education at Arizona State University. A widely known expert on fitness and health, he is author or co-author of 27 books addressed to students on those topics ranging from the elementary school through college. In August, 1986, he was given the "Better Health and Living Award" by that magazine as one of ten Americans who have made the difference in influencing others in the areas of health and fitness. He is a 1982 recipient of the National Honor Award from the American Alliance for Health, Physical Education, Recreation and Dance and is a fellow in the American Academy of Physical Education.

***Philip E. Allsen.*** Dr. Allsen is Professor of Physical Education and Director of the Fitness for Life Program at Brigham Young University in Provo, Utah. Widely known for his expertise in physical fitness, sports medicine, and athletic training, Dr. Allsen, a prolific writer, has authored more than 75 articles and written six books covering the topics of strength and physical fitness. The "Fitness for Life" program, which Dr. Allsen developed at Brigham Young University, now serves approximately 7,000 students at the institution each year and has been adopted by more than 400 schools in the United States. He is a member of the American College of Sports Medicine, the American Alliance of Health, Physical Education, Recreation and Dance, and the National Collegiate Physical Education Association.

# Preface

The purpose of *Bowling*, a volume in the SPORT FOR LIFE Series, is to help you learn to bowl, and to develop an enjoyment of the game. The book can be used as a text for class instruction or for learning the sport on your own. A large number of activities called "The Sport Experience" have been included to help you learn the concepts and develop the skills of bowling. Take time to do these activities as you read the book.

At the end of the book you will find Appendix A, a dictionary of bowling terms, Appendix B, a list of bowling resources, Appendix C, a test to check your learning, Appendix D, the answers to the problems and questions in the text, and Appendix E, a list of challenge activities for increasing your knowledge and expertise of bowling. These activities can be used in your bowling class or as independent learning aids.

## ACKNOWLEDGMENTS

We would like to give special thanks to Harriet Creed of Western Michigan University for her critical review of the manuscript and for allowing us to include many of her learning activities in the book. We also wish to thank J. Richard Jones; the SPORT FOR LIFE editors, Charles B. Corbin and Philip E. Allsen, for their encouragement and suggestions; and the Brunswick Company for the use of photographs of bowling lanes and equipment. The photographers for the book were Walter Cryer and John Durham.

Joyce M. Harrison<br>Ron Maxey

# Contents

## 1 How to Begin  1

Appropriate Dress for Bowling  1
Bowling Shoes  2
The Bowling Center  2
Bowling Balls  4
Other Equipment  8
Preconditioning and Warm-Ups  9
The History of Bowling  10
Benefits of Bowling  13

## 2 How to Become a Bowler  14

The Game  14
The Skills of the Game  16
    The One-Step Approach  17
    The Four-Step Approach  19
    The Three- and Five-Step Approaches  36
Practice and Feedback  39

## 3 Playing the Game  44

Scoring  44
Aiming Methods  51
Patterns of Ball Roll  53
Angle Adjustments for Strikes and Spares  58
Advanced Strategies  66

# 4 League and Tournament Play 71

**Bowling Leagues** 72
**Bowling Tournaments** 79

# 5 Strategies for the Advanced Bowler 85

**Reading the Lanes** 85
**Adjusting to Lane Conditions** 87
**Equipment Changes** 89

# 6 Playing the Mental Game 92

**Confidence** 93
**Compensation** 96

# 7 Where Do You Go from Here? 98

Appendix A  Bowling Dictionary  101
Appendix B  Bowling Resources  105
Appendix C  How Do You Stack Up?  106
Appendix D  Answers to Problems and Questions  114
Appendix E  Challenge Activities  117
Index  122

# How to Begin

Congratulations! You have just joined the top participant sport in the country. Bowling is a sport that can be enjoyed by people of all ages, both sexes, and varying skill levels. Whether you want to be a once-in-a-while bowler, a league bowler, or aim for the ranks of professional bowling, this book can start you off in the right direction. The SPORT FOR LIFE system is designed to teach everyone to bowl, regardless of ability. It uses a variety of learning activities and practice exercises to help you learn bowling at the level you wish to attain and to have fun while you are learning. Take time to do the Sport Experiences as you read the book. Good skills will follow. If you have difficulty with a new term, look it up in the bowling dictionary at the back of the book (Appendix A).

Included in the book are descriptions of appropriate dress and equipment, how to play the game, the skills and strategies of bowling, league and tournament bowling, the mental game, and how to continue the learning process. So what are we waiting for? Let's get started.

## *APPROPRIATE DRESS FOR BOWLING*

Bowling requires freedom of movement, so dress comfortably in short-sleeved shirts that allow considerable range of motion in the shoulder area and under the arms and in loose-fitting slacks. Avoid wearing tight pants or clothing that will draw your attention away from the game or interfere with the armswing or footwork.

**Appropriate dress for bowling**     **The bowling lanes**

## *BOWLING SHOES*

Choose bowling shoes in the same size as your street shoes. Bowling shoes for right-handed bowlers have a leather sole on the left shoe for sliding and a rubber tip on the right shoe for gripping. The soles of shoes for left-handed bowlers are reversed. Shoes rented at the bowling center have leather soles on both shoes and can be used by both right-handed and left-handed bowlers. If you bowl often, you will save money by buying your own shoes. You will also feel better in shoes that fit well and to which your feet are accustomed. Rented shoes are generally available only in medium widths which will not fit very narrow or very wide feet.

## *THE BOWLING CENTER*

As you enter the bowling center for the first time, you may feel like you're in a jungle of people and equipment, with strange sounds emanating from all sides. Just stand back and watch for a while and we'll help you sort it all out.

Every bowling center has a desk where you check in to receive a lane assignment. Sometimes you will have to wait to begin bowling until the players have finished a game on that lane. While you are waiting, let's learn about the equipment in a bowling center.

**Automatic pinspotters**

Each lane is divided into three sections—the pin area, the lane itself, and the approach. Behind the approach is a scoring table and a seating area. A *telescore* above the lane projects the score during league or tournament play to an overhead screen from a plastic scoresheet on the scoring table.

The *pin deck* supports ten pins, set 12 inches apart from center to center in a triangular shape. Each pin is approximately 5" across at its widest point and 15" high. Pins are usually made of wood covered with a thick plastic coating and weigh approximately 3 pounds 6 oz. each. The pins are numbered from one to ten as shown in the diagram. The number 1 pin is also called the *headpin* and the number 5 pin is called the *kingpin* because it is essential to the pin action in a strike. When the pins are hit they fly against side boards called *kickbacks* or against a

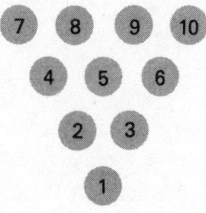

**Pin set-up**

*How to Begin*

*rear cushion* into a *pit*. An *automatic pinsetter* picks up the pins that remain after the first ball and respots them as they stand, even with their wobble. It also sends the ball back through the *ball return* which lies underground between every two lanes. The *rake* clears away *dead wood* (pins lying around) into the pit and the *pinsetter* respots the pins for the next ball. The *pin indicator*, above the pin deck, indicates which pins are left standing.

Each lane is 41-1/2 inches wide and 62-5/6 feet long, constructed of boards about one inch thick and three inches wide laid side-by-side on their edges. If you look closely, you can see where the hard maple boards on the ends dovetail into the softer pine boards in the middle of the lanes. Since the two ends of the lane receive the most abuse, the harder and more expensive maple boards are used under the pins and at the front of each lane.

A group of spots on the approach and arrows and spots on the lane help the bowler guide the approach and the release of the ball to get the best aim for knocking down pins.

The lane is separated from the approach by the *foul line*. A bowler stepping over the foul line loses all the pins knocked down on that ball. When an electric eye is breached, it activates an alarm and a light. However, the *foul lights* must be turned on for this to happen. They are usually on only during league or tournament play. Even if the foul light is not activated, however, it is good sportsmanship to call you own fouls.

The *approach* has markers twelve and fifteen feet from the foul line to help bowlers estimate a starting place for their approach. On the *ball return rack* are hand dryers to dry perspiring hands, a *reset button* to reset the pins when they are improperly set, and a *trouble button*. The trouble button is used to call the management for help when the pinsetter fails to respot the pins correctly or return the ball, or when pins are lying in the channels or on the lane too far away for the pinsetter to reach.

## *BOWLING BALLS*

Bowling balls come in hard rubber or various plastic materials in a variety of colors. All balls have a maximum weight of sixteen pounds and a circumference of not more than twenty-seven inches. They are approximately eight and one-half inches in diameter. Although balls come in eight to sixteen pound weights, some automatic pinsetters

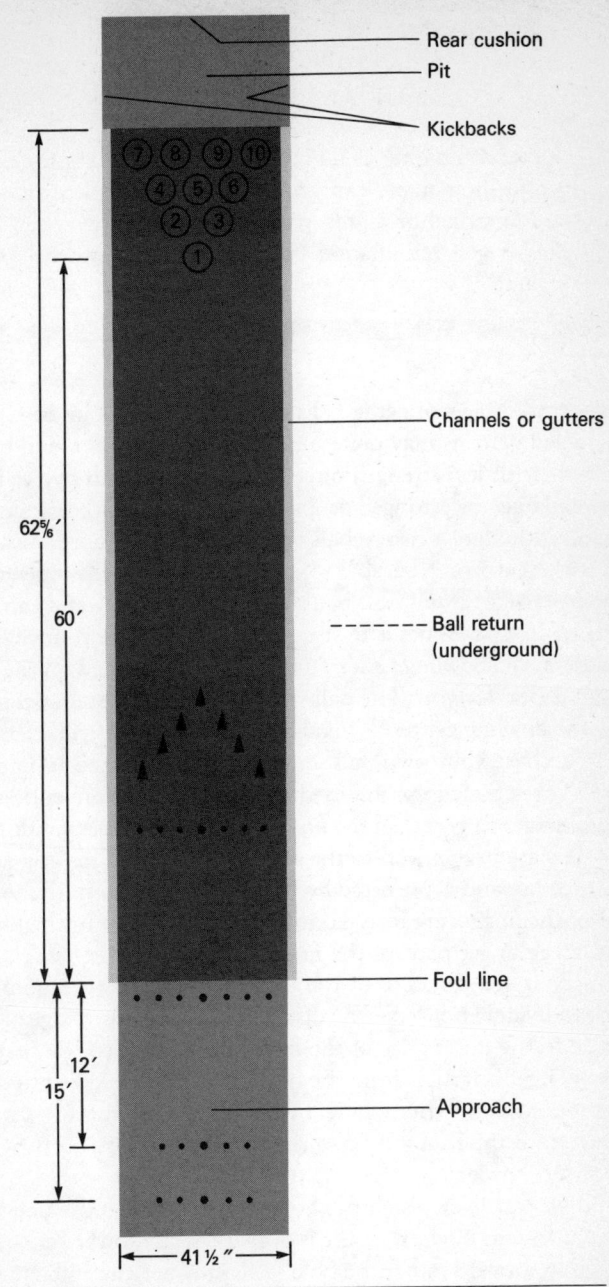

**The lane**

*How to Begin* 5

## THE SPORT EXPERIENCE

Spend some time at a bowling center watching the bowlers. Notice how many can knock down all ten pins with one ball (a strike) or all ten pins with two balls (a spare). Each bowler gets ten chances (frames) of one or two balls each in a game.

---

have difficulty managing balls of less than ten pounds. Children and disabled persons may prefer using an eight to ten pound ball. Smaller people with less strength often start with a ten to twelve pound ball, while larger or stronger people usually begin with a fourteen pound ball. Although a heavy ball will knock down more pins, if it is too heavy, you won't be able to control it so it will hinder rather than help. The key is to find a ball that fits comfortably and can be handled easily. Your best bet is to use a *house ball*, which you will find on the racks in the bowling center, until you have decided on the ball weight that is best for you. The ball weight is generally stamped on each ball at the bowling center. If you bowl regularly, you will eventually want to purchase your own ball so that it can be drilled to fit your hand.

Three basic grips are used by bowlers—the conventional grip, the semi-fingertip grip, and the fingertip grip. In the conventional grip, the fingers are inserted up to the second knuckles. This grip is the easiest one to use and is preferred by beginning bowlers. In the semi-fingertip grip, the fingers are inserted to the first knuckles. In the fingertip grip, only the finger pads of the fingers hold on to the ball.

Balls are drilled to fit the three basic grips, with minor variations for individual bowlers. The distance from the inner edge of the thumbhole to the inner edge of the finger holes is called the *span*. Since the ring finger is farther from the thumb than the middle finger, its hole is farther from the thumbhole. In house balls the finger holes are equidistant from the thumbhole so they can be used by both right and left-handed bowlers.

The angle at which the holes are drilled into the ball is called the *pitch*. In zero pitch, the hole is drilled directly toward the center of the ball. In forward pitch, the hole angles toward the emblem on the ball; in reverse pitch it angles away from the emblem. In lateral pitch, the

## THE SPORT EXPERIENCE

Go to a bowling center and locate a ball that meets the following criteria:

1. The thumb turns easily in the thumbhole without sticking, but the hole is not so big that you have to grip the ball to hang on to it.

2. With your thumb in the thumbhole and your hand flat on the ball, the second knuckles of the middle two fingers extend one-fourth inch beyond the inside edge of the finger holes.

3. With your thumb and fingers in the ball, one lead pencil will fit between your hand and the ball. More than one pencil indicates the holes are too close together. If no pencil fits, the holes are too far apart.

---

hole angles off to the side of the thumb—left of the emblem is left pitch and right of the emblem is right pitch (Pezzano, Chuck, *Professional Bowlers Association Guide to Better Bowling*. New York: Simon and Schuster, Inc., 1983, p. 44).

The standard pitch for a beginning bowler is usually a forward pitch, three-eighths inch above the center of the ball. However, since

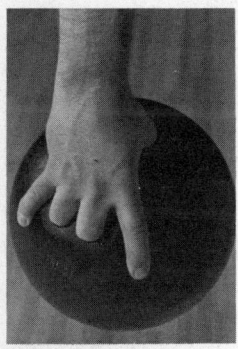
Conventional

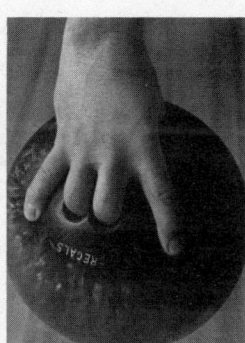
Semi-fingertip

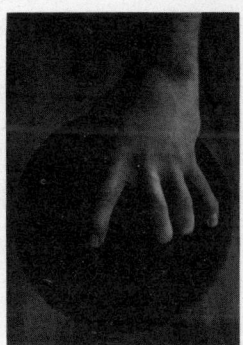
Fingertip

**Bowling grips**

*How to Begin*

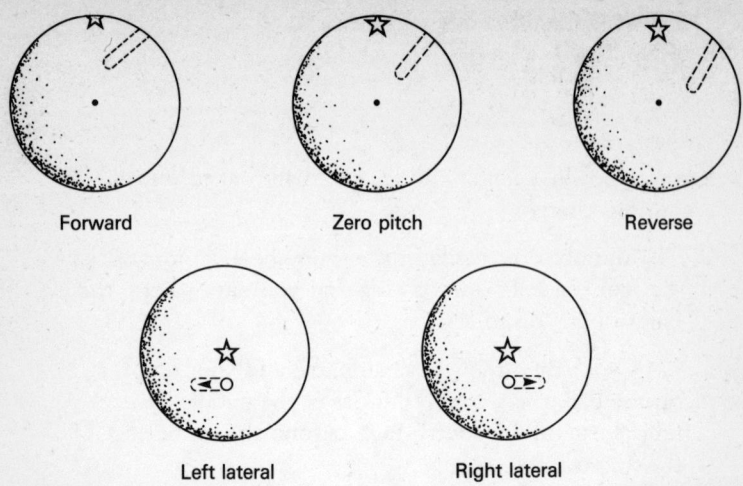

**Ball pitch (note location of emblem and center of ball in relation to each pitch)**

everyone's hands are different, care should be taken to fit the pitch to the actual bowler's hand.

The shells of bowling balls vary in hardness. The harder the coating, the less the ball will hook toward the pins as it rolls down the lane. The softer the ball, the more it will grip the lane and hook toward the pins. This may be important if you have difficulty with your hook ball later on.

## *OTHER EQUIPMENT*

The selection of bowling equipment could be limited to a ball and shoes or it could include a large number of bowling accessories. You will need a bag to carry your ball and shoes when you purchase your own equipment. You will find a towel valuable for removing moisture from your hands and oil and dirt from your ball and shoes. Many bowlers use a wrist support to help maintain a straight wrist. Carry a roll of tape to adjust the size of the holes in your ball and a knife or scissors to cut the tape. Include an extra pair of shoelaces. A rosin bag or some other type of powder can be used to help your grip. Sandpaper is used to make adjustments to your ball surface and holes. First-aid supplies and fingernail clippers can be used to treat injuries, especially to your fingers or thumb. Clippers can also be used to keep calluses trimmed down. It is wise to keep the fingers free of excessively

**Bowling equipment**

**Warm-up exercises**

hardened skin or damaged nails. There are other accessories, but this list will make you aware that you may want more than a ball and shoes for your bowling equipment.

## *PRECONDITIONING AND WARM-UPS*

Conditioning for bowling should begin with a general body conditioning program. Cardiovascular endurance can be developed by sustained, continuous movement exercises that utilize large-muscle groups. Activities such as aerobics, jogging, swimming, dance, and the martial arts can be used to increase cardiovascular endurance. Muscular strength and endurance can be developed through the use of weight training or with exercises such as pushups, chinups, or bar dips for the chest, shoulders, and back muscles. Exercises such as jumping and running should adequately strengthen the legs. High repetitions of strength development exercises are great for developing muscular endurance.

In addition to a general fitness program, specific exercises can be used to develop the muscle groups involved in the execution of bowl-

## THE SPORT EXPERIENCE

Practice the following exercises to prepare yourself for bowling:

1. Warm up your arms by swinging the arms backward and forward in a pendulum swing and by doing arm circles.

2. Stretch the leg muscles by taking a long stride forward, then lean forward over the front foot until a slight stretch "pain" is felt in the back leg. Repeat with the opposite leg.

3. Do some slow toe touches.

4. Strengthen your wrists by doing the following: Tie a weight to the end of a rope and the opposite end of the rope to the middle of your broom handle. Now, place your hands palms down on each end of the broomstick and roll it in your hands until the rope is wound up. Reverse your hands to a palms up position and roll the broomstick toward you to unwind the rope.

---

ing skills. Right-handed bowlers should especially strengthen the right hand, arm, and shoulder, and the left leg. Critical to great skill in bowling is a wrist strong enough to execute a powerful release. To strengthen the wrist, one must develop the muscles of the forearm.

The best warm-up exercises for bowling are flexibility exercises and bowling itself. The exercises are done to stretch the leg and shoulder muscles. After the exercises, bowl a few frames to warm-up.

## THE HISTORY OF BOWLING

The first bowlers may have been stone age men who rolled rocks at pointed stones or at enemies.

Sir Flinders Petrie, a British Egyptologist, discovered implements for a bowling-type game in the tomb of a child buried about 5200 B.C.

"The Game of Skittles" by Pieter de Hooch (ca. 1665)

(Hovis, Ford, editor, *The Sports Encyclopedia*. New York: Praeger Publishers, Inc., 1976, p. 58).

Early Polynesians played a game called *Ula Moika* in which small balls were bowled sixty feet at flat stone disks.

Some bowling historians claim that the earliest European bowlers were the Helvetti, inhabitants of the alpine regions of northern Italy during Caesar's time (circa 50 B.C.). The game apparently evolved into the present-day Italian game of *boccie*.

The earliest pin bowling may have occurred in the cloisters of cathedrals, according to the ancient chronicles of Paderborn (Menke, Frank G., *Encyclopedia of Sports*. New York: A. S. Barnes and Company, 1944, p. 156). In the third century A.D., each parishioner carried a club (like an Indian club) called a *kegel* for protection and was directed to bowl a stone at his kegel, which represented the devil or the heathen. Success indicated a clean life, while failure demonstrated a need for more faithful attendance at church services.

*How to Begin*

Later, the monks grouped the pins and took turns with the ball. Wooden balls soon replaced pebbles and the shapes of the pins were modified. Bowling soon spread from the churches to the upper classes and became very popular in Germany. Wealthy Germans had bowling lanes on their estates or in their palaces. Village celebrations included bowling. However, much confusion existed as to the number of pins to be used in the game and the formation for setting them up.

In the fifteenth century, Martin Luther standardized the rules of bowling, setting the number of pins at nine—three rows of three pins each in a diamond shape. Indoor ninepin games were played by rolling the ball. In outdoor games, the ball could be rolled or thrown at the pins.

Nearly every European country had its own form of bowling. These games included ninepins in Holland, skittles and bowles in England, road bowling in Ireland, curling (on ice) in Scotland, and carreau and quilles in France. The word *bowl* is found in all northern European languages.

Bowling became so popular in England that King Edward III in 1366 outlawed the sport because it was interfering with the practice of archery, an essential military skill. Sir Francis Drake, the famous British admiral, when notified of the approach of the Spanish Armada off the coast of England (1588), insisted he had time both to complete his bowling game and to destroy the Armada.

Ninepins was brought to America by the Dutch settlers of Manhattan Island in the 1600s. In *Rip Van Winkle*, Washington Irving mentioned the "rumbling peals of thunder" caused by balls hitting pins.

By the middle 1800s, in spite of Puritan disapproval, ninepins was popular in New York. The Knickerbocker Alleys opened as the first indoor lanes in the United States, with clay floors. Gambling, however, was rampant and the Connecticut legislature outlawed the game in 1841.

Later, according to legend, some unknown person added a tenth pin, thus circumventing the law, and ten-pin bowling became rapidly accepted, with the set-up changed from a diamond to the present triangle. In 1895, the American Bowling Congress standardized the rules of bowling and rapid growth occurred thereafter. With the advent of the World Wars and the formation of the Women's International Bowling Congress, women's bowling increased dramatically and bowling operators cleaned up their establishments and began catering to people of both sexes and all ages. The automatic pinsetter moder-

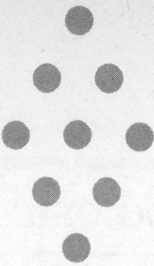

**Ninepin set-up**

nized bowling and led to the development of large bowling centers for family bowling. Bowling is now a very popular family activity. It is also particularly adaptable to participation by disabled persons. A guide rail for blind bowlers is available in many centers.

## BENEFITS OF BOWLING

Bowling can offer you a number of benefits. One of the greatest benefits of bowling is the development of friendships. Bowling is a social activity which will result in friendships if you interact socially with other bowlers. Another benefit is the relaxation provided by engaging in a physical activity.

Two challenges that you may have to overcome, if you have not already done so, include dealing with competition and working effectively with others. Overcoming these challenges will help you develop the ability to overcome other obstacles in your life.

For a few people, bowling can also be rewarding monetarily. Highly skilled bowlers can make money through competitive bowling. Bowling centers, instructors, and pro shops also make money. As you can see, the benefits of bowling are determined by what you personally want to achieve.

# How to Become a Bowler

Although most players learn to bowl by going to a bowling center with a group of friends, that may not be the most effective way for you to learn. The reason is that imitating incorrect skills and concepts can lead to learning the wrong things. The best way, of course, is to obtain a teacher who can provide you with correct information and skills. However, a good teacher is not always available, so this chapter will allow you to get a good start on your own.

## THE GAME

A bowling game is called a *line*, perhaps because each person's game consists of one line on a bowling scoresheet. The purpose of the game is to knock down all ten pins in each of ten frames represented by boxes on the scoresheet.

One or two balls are rolled in each frame. A bonus is awarded for knocking down all ten pins with two balls (a spare) and a double bonus is given for doing so with only one ball (a strike). In a perfect game of 300 points, the player gets twelve strikes in a row, with 30 points in each frame.

Each sport has its own code of etiquette. When you begin bowling, you will want to conduct yourself appropriately. Bowling etiquette generally consists of common sense plus common courtesy. The basic rules of bowling etiquette include the following:

1. Check in at the desk and wait your turn for a lane.
2. Select a ball from the racks and return it to its place upon finishing. Learn to identify your own ball.
3. Never use another player's ball without permission.
4. Use proper equipment—ball, shoes, etc. Put on bowling shoes before entering the bowling area.
5. Be ready to bowl when your turn comes.
6. When two people are on the approach, the player on the right has the right-of-way.
7. Keep your "body English" in your own lane. Movements of the body following the release can be distracting to bowlers on adjoining lanes.
8. Remain behind the foul lines.
9. Stand behind the approach while awaiting the return of your ball. Never roll a second ball until the first one has been returned. It may break the pinsetter.
10. Return immediately after bowling to the rear of the approach and remain seated until your next turn.
11. Keep your advice to yourself unless you are asked.
12. Never speak to a bowler who has taken his or her stance.
13. Learn the rules of the game.
14. Don't alibi—Be a good winner or a good loser. Watch your language and temper.
15. In short, be courteous at all times.

Safety in bowling is of paramount importance. Bruised fingers or torn muscles resulting from improper safety with balls, lanes, and shoes can temporarily handicap you or others. Some safety rules every bowler should follow include the ones listed below:

1. Wear appropriate clothing and accessories.
2. Use a correctly fitting ball.

3. Pick up the ball with both hands *after* it has stopped moving.
4. Grasp the ball on the sides to prevent the fingers from being crushed.
5. Use clean, dry shoe soles to prevent slipping. Substances such as pumice, powder, or resin are prohibited because they might injure the lane surface.
6. If the approach is slippery or sticky, notify the management.
7. Keep food and drinks away from the bowling area. For safety and courtesy, eating and drinking should be confined to the seating area.
8. Be careful with practice swings.

## THE SKILLS OF THE GAME

Now that you have an idea of how the game of bowling is played, let's examine, one at a time, the skills that will allow you to be successful in your bowling adventure. Most people believe that bowling is easy and anyone can do it. It is true that most people can roll the ball down the lane but it is an entirely different matter to roll the ball down the lane accurately and with consistently effective power. The skills needed to do this include the four-step approach (footwork) and armswing. After each skill is described, a series of learning activities will be provided to

Stance

Pushaway

Backswing

**One-step approach**

# THE SPORT EXPERIENCE

Review the etiquette and safety factors with a friend. Explain why you think each item is important.

---

help you more fully understand how to utilize the information to improve your skills and scores in bowling. Ways to evaluate your effectiveness will also be presented. The text is presented from the point-of-view of a right-handed bowler. The basic principles and movements are the same for right or left-handed bowlers. Minor differences occur in the approach and delivery. Differences in adapting to lane conditions are discussed in Chapter 5. Good luck in your pursuit of the mastery of bowling!

## The One-Step Approach

The one-step approach and delivery is a preliminary exercise to all bowling approaches. Stand, facing the pins, about four or five feet from the foul line for this exercise. Lift the ball with both hands and place it in front of your chest. Now practice only the swing. Push the ball down and forward. When the ball is forward and the arms are ex-

**Release**

tended at the elbows, allow the ball to swing past your body and upward behind your shoulder. The nondominant hand should be removed just before the ball starts down and back. With a relaxed continuous swing, allow the ball to swing down and forward and catch it in front of your chest. Repeat this a few times. This is an excellent warmup before bowling, even for a skilled bowler. Another good warmup is to swing the arm, without the ball, around in a complete circle.

Now the swing will be done with a one-step delivery. Stand one long step away from the foul line (or imaginary foul line). Place both feet together in a natural stance. Hold the ball in a "shake-hands" grip in front of your chest. Focus your eyes on a target such as the second arrow from the ball channel on your dominant-hand side. Push the ball forward, down, and to the dominant-hand side of the body. The posture should remain erect in this position. The ball now swings down and back in a pendulum motion. The swing continues until the top of the backswing is reached. Bend forward from the waist at the beginning of the backswing. The ball will now swing down and forward. As it does, allow the arm to relax and move in a smooth flowing manner. Step out with the nondominant foot. Place the toe down and slide forward. Finish the slide by placing the heel down at the finish of the downward and forward movement of the ball or armswing. Release your hand from the ball as your hand starts upward. Keep the arm in the natural hanging position and lift the arm upward until the

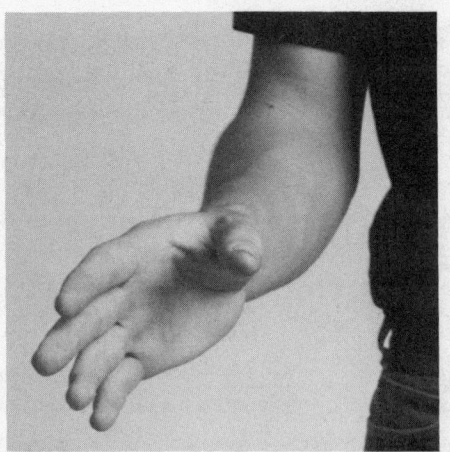

**Shake-hands grip**

# THE SPORT EXPERIENCE

Master the one-step approach on the lane before reading further. Remember:

1. Use the "shake-hands" grip from the beginning to the release.

2. Focus the eys on the target arrow (the second arrow from the channel).

3. Draw a diagram of the path of the ball on the lane and record the number of times the ball stayed on the lane *or* the number of pins knocked down.

---

elbow stops beside the head. This completes the one-step delivery. The one-step approach is a good delivery for many handicapped bowlers to use.

Practice the one-step approach without the ball first so you understand exactly what to do when you practice with the ball. In this chapter we have included many learning activities. If you do the activities as they are presented, you will learn the game of bowling; so take time now to practice the one-step approach.

## The Four-Step Approach

Before analyzing each step of the approach and each phase of the armswing, let's walk through the entire four-step approach in order to get a picture of the whole. The following description is for a right-handed bowler. If you bowl left-handed, simply use the opposite feet from those described.

While doing the same armswing as in the one-step delivery, step forward with the right foot as you push the ball down, forward, and to the right. Step with the left foot and let the ball swing back and down. Step with the right foot and complete the backswing. Slide with the left foot. Swing the ball forward and down. Plant the left foot and release the ball out on to the lane. Lift your right arm up beside your head.

*How to Become a Bowler*

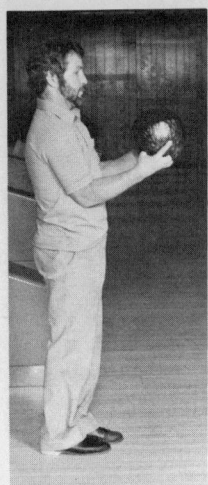 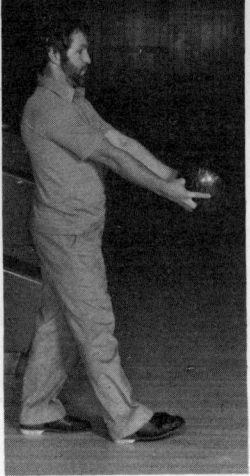 

Stance　　　Pushaway　　　Downswing

**Four-step approach**

***The Footwork.*** Basic to building a good foundation in bowling is to understand how to have great footwork and to practice until you have it firmly established in your neuromuscular pathways. By utilizing the ideas presented in this section, the footwork in your bowling approach can become as easy and as consistent as walking down the street. Strive for consistency.

Essential to good footwork is the ability to walk in a straight line. The bowling lanes are made of boards that run from the end of the ap-

Attempt a few deliveries to become familiar with the four-step approach and armswing. Do not worry about the number of pins down at this point. Concentrate on a smooth approach and swing. Focus your eyes on the second arrow from the gutter and try to roll the ball over that arrow. An instructor, if you have one, can watch and become familiar with your body movements.

proach to the pit behind the pins. These boards are basically straight. Learn to walk straight down the boards. A right-handed bowler, for example, should practice walking so the left foot stays on the same board on the second and fourth steps of the four-step approach. Most bowling lanes have dots on the approach to help you continue to step on the same board. Another method is to use the differences in the coloration of the boards to help you make the alignment. If your bowling center will allow it, run a piece of tape along the board or color the board with chalk, making it very easy to see. If the proprietor will not allow this, you can measure the approach and put the tape down at home. One disadvantage at home is that the sliding surface is usually different on your carpet, tile, or other home floor covering. You can practice walking straight without any expenditure of money. This point can not be overemphasized. Development of skill in walking in a straight line is the first step to good footwork.

The next essential to mastery of your footwork is to learn to be consistent with the length and placement of each step in your approach. The first step should be the shortest and the last step the longest. The slide that accompanies the last step is the main factor that lengthens the last step. Each step should be progressivly longer than the one before it. The reason for increased length is that the ball travels a greater distance on each step. The ball moves faster on step two than on step one and much faster on step four than on step three.

The fact that the ball stops at the top of the backswing makes it extremely important to use the third step as a timing step. The checkpoint for timing is to have the backswing completed as you complete your third step. Because of the distance the ball must travel, you may want to have the ball start forward slightly before your body momentum carries you into the fourth step. It is very effective in solving timing problems if you can learn to control your steps in relation to the armswing and ball movement. It will also help your release because you will have a slow, steady footwork, which is essential to good timing. Timing and body position are necessary to good balance or stability at the release.

The placement of the feet or method of stepping is another important consideration. As simple as it may appear, it is important to understand that the first three steps should be heel-toe steps and the fourth step should be a toe-slide-heel step. The first three steps should be as close to natural walking steps as possible. Most people walk with a heel-toe stepping pattern as opposed to a toe-heel step. The first three steps are necessary to transport you toward the foul line and pins

# THE SPORT EXPERIENCE

Practice the footwork of the four-step approach on the lane. Use the checklist under *"The Error Corrector"* (p. 26) to analyze your footwork.

---

while your armswing creates a smooth flowing momentum preparatory to the release of the ball from your hand.

The fourth step is your power step. The body slides forward and downward in a powerful manner to transfer the body's energy into the ball at the point of release. The leg should end in a bent-knee position. The angle of bend may be determined by whether you plant your heel prior to or after the release. Some great bowlers plant their heel prior to release and some after the release. Either way can be effective. The important thing is to develop one method or the other so your timing and balance are consistent at the release. The heel plant-then release method is effectively used by bowlers who have a tendency to get their feet slightly ahead of the armswing. However, this can be a serious er-

**Picking up the ball safely**

**Footwork**

*How to Become a Bowler*　　　　　　　　　　　　　　　　　　　　　　　23

ror for many bowlers because they get so far ahead of the ball that they become off-balanced or have to rush the last part of the swing. Rushing the swing almost always results in a lack of balance and a poor release. To avoid this problem, strive to release the ball before or at the same time as you plant the heel.

**The Address.** Each time a ball is rolled down the lane, it is preceded by an address to the pins. Addressing the pins starts when you leave your seat or standing position to go pick up your ball from the ball return machine. The moment you start your address your mental and physical activity play a critical role to your success in that frame. Learn to have successful frames. Bowling games or tournaments are won as a result of a series of successful frames, so think only of one frame at a time. It is good to shut everything out of your mind except your actions and attitudes related to bowling the ball or frame at hand. Make the address disciplined and consistent. This will help establish habits and attitudes that may determine your success or failure as a bowler.

Your approach has begun. Walk quietly and orderly to the ball return rack. Bend over and lift your ball with both hands. Place your hands so they are not between the balls. Keep your eyes on the balls so you don't have several balls roll together and smash your fingers. Injuries to fingers have a tendency to reduce scores.

To determine your starting position, walk to the foul line. Turn so your back is toward the pins. Walk forward four-and-one-half or five steps. Turn and face the pins. For a beginning position stand slightly to the right of the center of the lane. You are now in your starting position. Remember where you position yourself so you can repeat it each time you bowl. Stand with your feet together, weight balanced, ready to step out on the right foot. Bend your knees a little. Be comfortable and stay relaxed.

Lift your ball in front of your waist with both hands, using a "shake-hands" grip. Place the right elbow close to your body, which will line the ball up with the shoulder. This will help you develop a straight pendulum swing. Position your shoulders so they are square to the target. Keep them square throughout your approach. Use both hands to hold the ball, with the weight of the ball supported by the nondominant hand. Keep the wrist of the bowling arm in a firm, straight position. Look at the target arrow on the lane. Your eyes should remain on this spot until the ball rolls over it.

There are a number of techniques for holding the ball in prepara-

Assume the correct stance in front of a mirror and check for errors using The Error Corrector checklist (p. 27) *or* have a partner analyze your stance using the checklist.

tion for your approach. These will be discussed in the section on the pushaway. Once you have taken your position, your address to the pins is over.

**The Armswing.** Now it is time to learn the important aspects of the armswing. For consistent delivery, the armswing must travel in the same basic pattern each time the ball is rolled toward the pins. Understanding and developing a consistent pendulum armswing will make it much easier to adjust the footwork to the armswing. Development of good basic skills such as a smooth pendulum swing with the footwork perfectly timed to the armswing will improve scores.

Practice the armswing both mentally and physically. Mental practice will help you establish clearly in your mind what you are attempting to do. Go over each aspect of the armswing in your mind before you go on the lanes. This has at least two advantages. First, you know exactly what you will do during your practice time before you pick up the ball. You will not experiment as much, which is good because bad habits often occur when experimenting. Second, you won't waste your money fooling around. Fool around off the lanes. Bowl when you get on the lanes if you desire to improve your bowling skills. Make it enjoyable but don't waste your time or money.

The armswing can be divided into six parts—the pushaway, downswing, backswing, forward swing, release, and follow-through. Although it is one continuous swing, each part is critical to excellent timing. Timing is coordinating the footwork with the armswing. If errors exist in the armswing it becomes very difficult, if not impossible, to adjust the footwork to the armswing. Therefore, strive to understand and practice the following points about the armswing.

**The Pushaway.** The initial movement in the armswing is the pushaway, which is critical to the total timing of the approach. The

# THE ERROR CORRECTOR

## Footwork Errors and Corrections

*Steps not in straight line to target*
> Practice walking straight down one board.

*Steps too long or too short*
> Make your first step the shortest and make each step longer than the one before.

*Steps too fast*
> Slow down the feet.

*Using the wrong foot to slide*
> Right-handed bowlers start on the right foot, take four steps, and slide on the left foot.

**Starting ball positions for pushaway**

# THE ERROR CORRECTOR

## Stance Errors and Corrections

*No bend in knees, increases tension and makes it harder to take the first step*
> Practice different degrees of bend to find your most comfortable stance. Some bowlers use bounce to settle into their stance.

*Shoulders not square to target. This error can exist throughout the approach and delivery.*
> Concentrate on your shoulder position before starting the pushaway. Keep the shoulders square to the target at all times during your approach and delivery.

*Elbow away from the side*
> Tuck your elbow into the body.

*Variable stance position. This will affect your aim.*
> Stand in the same position on the approach for each strike.

*Eyes off the target making it hard to hit the target.*
> Before starting the pushaway, decide on your spot and keep your eyes on it until the ball rolls over it.

---

three positions most highly recommended and effective for the pushaway are the high, middle, and low starting positions.

In the high position, the ball is placed at chest level. This is desirable when the bowler is attempting to increase the speed of the ball by lengthening the swing, rather than through increased strength, improved timing, or a faster approach. The ball is usually positioned in the center of the body, so the bowler should push the ball down and to the right to align the ball with the right shoulder. This assures

# THE SPORT EXPERIENCE

Practice the pushaway utilizing the following activities:

1. Practice the pushaway without stepping, using each of the three starting positions. Use good body posture. Test your control of the ball on the pushaway. The lack of control can result from poor body posture or a lack of strength. Lack of strength can be eliminated by choosing a lighter ball or by strengthening your body. Continual practice of this exercise will provide some increase in strength. If you have a serious strength problem and desire to become a skilled bowler, start a strength program.

2. Practice the pushaway and first step alone. The pushaway should be completed as the heel of the first step touches down. Regular practice of the pushaway is important in the development of good timing in the total approach and delivery.

3. An excellent method for practicing these two pushaway exercises is to have someone help you control the weight of the ball. The helper should stand to your right and one or two feet away, positioned so only the arms have to move. It is more clumsy if the helper has to move to meet the ball. The helper places both hands under the ball and guides you through the pushaway. Strive to develop a sense of timing which will allow you to start the ball in motion prior to the foot movement and complete the pushaway as the heel of the foot touches down. Practice a few times with your helper, then practice with the helper observing. A qualified instructor may be most helpful, but anyone who understands the exercise and desires to help you can do an excellent job. These exercises should increase your ability to control the ball when you execute the pushaway alone.

4. Practice the pushaway and first step. Check yourself using The Error Corrector checklist.

# THE ERROR CORRECTOR

## Pushaway Errors and Their Corrections

*Ball pushed up instead of down*
> Practice the pushaway without stepping. Practice the exercise with the helper. Concentrate on pushing the ball down and forward.

*Ball dropped, eliminates the pendulum*
> Reread the section on the pushaway. Practice fully extending the pushaway.

*Too much right or left movement on pushaway, eliminates pendulum and disrupts balance*
> Align the ball with the shoulder and elbow. Tuck the elbow into the body below the shoulder. From this starting position practice the armswing. Stand before a mirror to see if the swing is in line with the shoulder and in a front to back direction throughout the swing.

*Ball pushed out too far, destroys balance*
> Keep the shoulders square to the target. When you push away, don't extend the shoulder.

*Ball moves after the first step, causes poor timing*
> Place the ball against your body in the starting position. Practice moving the ball down and forward until the elbow passes the body, then step as the pushaway is completed. Practice only the pushaway five or ten times, then do the complete approach.

*Nonbowling hand released too late or too soon. Too soon prevents relaxation of bowling arm; too late causes the shoulders to turn in order to keep the ball from hitting your leg.*
> Allow your hands to separate as the ball starts the downswing.

that the ball will be in the straight-under-the-shoulder pendulum swing when the ball enters the downswing. It is extremely important that this alignment occur prior to the downswing. If it doesn't it will cause balance problems and make it difficult to get a straight swing. When the balance is disrupted, it becomes very difficult to regain it until after the ball leaves the hand. To use this position you need to develop a graceful flowing approach. If you tend to be rigid and methodical, you should choose the middle or low starting position.

The middle or waist-level position is the most desirable for beginning bowlers. Adjustments to a higher or lower position can come easier than adjusting from the extremes. To establish the middle position with the ball in the right hand, place the ball just in front of the body, half way between the right hip and right shoulder. By placing the ball to the outside of the body the pushaway will be in line with the pendulum swing. Eliminating the need for adjustments helps maintain a straight, balanced, and relaxed swing.

To shorten the pushaway, which helps with timing, the right elbow rather than the hand can be placed above the hip. The middle position can be extended so the pushaway is completed before any steps have been taken. This is advisable only when the bowler has great difficulty establishing proper timing between the pushaway and the first step.

The low position is established by letting the arm extend naturally and by placing the ball in front and to the side of the right thigh. The pushaway becomes a slight push up and forward on the first step. This is used most often when the bowler desires a slightly bent posture, which is assumed with a forward bend from the waist. Sometimes it helps bowlers eliminate pushaway problems they have in another starting posture.

The choice of starting position is not critical to a successful pushaway. However, the ball position can make a difference in the timing of the approach and in the speed of the ball. The critical aspect of the pushaway is to have it completed as the heel of the first step contacts the approach. Proper movement of the ball and the maintenance of good posture are important to the timing between the foot and the hand or ball.

The ball should be in motion prior to the movement of the first step. As the ball starts forward the first step should occur. The ball should move forward, down, and to the dominant side of the body. There is an exception to the ball being in motion first. That occurs when the pushaway has been eliminated by extending the starting position. But in essence you did move the ball first. The exception is that the armswing isn't continuous. The pushaway occurs. The ball stops. The first step is taken. The ball then starts again as the first step is completed and the second step begins. This technique can result in a lower ball speed.

The posture should be erect before the pushaway begins and remain erect until the pushaway is completed. As the ball moves forward and the elbow extends, the shoulder should not extend. If the shoulder extends it is more difficult to control the weight of the ball. The lack of ball control causes loss of posture, which results in a loss of balance. Loss of balance in the pushaway could result in a loss of balance throughout the entire approach and delivery. Don't allow the shoulder blades to separate during the pushaway. This will help keep the shoulders aligned. A contraction and an arching of the lower back will help keep the posture very erect.

***The Downswing.*** The downswing requires less effort than any other part of the armswing. That doesn't mean it is less important. If the bowler is relaxed and has good command of the pushaway, the position of the ball in relation to step two should be excellent. The shoulder of the bowling arm should be as relaxed as possible. This will help the ball move freely into the downswing and pendulum swing. The pendulum is created when the ball passes close to the body and directly under the shoulder. The left hand should leave the ball at the beginning of the downswing. The ball should move into the downswing as the toe of the right foot is planted in step one.

At the completion of the downswing, the right arm and ball should be aligned with the right shoulder and hip. It is difficult to check this point because the ball is moving past the body into the backswing and you cannot see the position of the ball at the end of this step. Stopping is impractical because the flow of the swing would be interrupted. It is also very difficult to correct it by feel because what you become accustomed to feels right. A qualified instructor can see the position of the ball in the pushaway and the backswing and can tell if the follow-through is positioned well. These three positions have a pause that makes them easier to analyze. Because of the difficulty analyzing the downswing, you should concentrate more on the pushaway and the backswing.

***The Backswing.*** The backswing flows immediately out of the downswing. It might also be considered the upswing of the pendulum.

# THE SPORT EXPERIENCE

Practice the pushaway activities you learned previously to help you with proper ball positioning on the downswing. Proper ball position will prevent the weight of the ball from pulling you off-balance as you enter the downswing.

1. Practice the pushaway without stepping, using each of the three starting positions. Use good body posture. Test your control of the ball on the pushaway. The lack of control can result from poor body posture or a lack of strength. Lack of strength can be eliminated by choosing a lighter ball or by strengthening your body. Continual practice of this exercise will provide some increase in strength.

2. Practice the pushaway and first step alone. The pushaway should be completed as the heel of the first step touches down. Regular practice of the pushaway is important in the development of good timing in the total approach and delivery.

3. An excellent method for practicing these two pushaway exercises is to have someone help you control the weight of the ball. The helper should stand to your right and one or two feet away, positioned so only the arms have to move. It is more clumsy if the helper has to move to meet the ball. The helper places both hands under the ball and guides you through the pushaway. Strive to develop a sense of timing which will allow you to start the ball in motion prior to the foot movement and complete the pushaway as the heel of the foot touches down. Practice a few times with your helper, then practice with the helper observing.

## THE SPORT EXPERIENCE

Practice the following activities to help you improve your backswing:

1. Extend the arm fully on the pushaway and end the pushaway with the ball directly in line with its intended arc. The ball and arm should swing freely like a pendulum from the shoulder. Keep your shoulders square to the target.

2. To prevent the problem of stopping the ball at the top of the backswing, stand in a natural stance and let the arm and ball hang at your side. Push the ball forward similar to the low starting position pushaway. Eliminate the first two steps so you can concentrate on getting the ball immediately out of the backswing. Allow the ball to move through the pushaway and downswing. As the ball passes the body, step on the heel of the third step. As soon as the heel touches the ground, swing the ball forward.

3. Check your backswing using The Error Corrector checklist (p. 34).

---

The two serious points to consider in the backswing are the alignment of the shoulders and the position of the third step. The shoulders should be square to the target at the beginning of the third step and should stay facing the target throughout the entire delivery. Problems result from opening the shoulders, resulting in an excessively high backswing, or moving the ball around the hip in a circular pattern rather than in a straight pendulum swing. Pausing at the top of the backswing results from incorrect timing of the armswing and footwork.

**The Forward Swing.** The forward swing is from the top of the backswing to the point of release. The swing should begin as the weight of the body transfers from the heel to the toe of the third step.

## THE ERROR CORRECTOR

### Backswing Errors and Their Corrections

*Backswing away from the body*
> Keep the ball close to the body as it passes your hip.

*Backswing goes behind your back*
> Keep your shoulders and hips square to your target. Push the ball to the dominant side so the ball is in front of its intended arc. Keep the shoulder over the intended arc of the ball.

*Ball stops at top of backswing*
> Start the ball forward as the third step is completed.

*Backswing too high caused by opening the shoulders*
> Lower the backswing slightly and concentrate on keeping the shoulders square to the target.

---

The ball travels approximately the distance of the downswing and backswing combined. Because of the distance traveled, the bowler needs to use part of the third step to equalize the steps to the distance traveled. Therefore, starting the ball forward at the correct time is critical.

The most serious problems on the forward swing are forcing the ball forward through muscle action and a lack of balance prior to, during, and after the release. If the pushaway, downswing, and backswing are properly executed, then the balance problem should be solved unless it is due to a weak, tired, or poorly positioned last step.

**The Release.** The release is the point in the approach and delivery when the ball leaves your fingers. It is the source of that kind of ball roll necessary for effective pin action or strike power. When properly executed, it is the secret to a powerful strike ball. It should be done with lift and a squeezing action of the fingers.

# THE SPORT EXPERIENCE

Practice the following activities to improve your forward swing:

1. Use a ball that is light enough to control. A heavier ball that is uncontrolled will lower your scores, rather than improving them. A light ball will also make it easier to relax, which will help your timing and balance.

2. Relax and allow the pendulum swing to increase your ball velocity, rather than attempting to increase velocity through increased muscular force. If you must increase muscular force, do it during your follow-through.

3. Analyze your forward swing using The Error Corrector checklist.

# THE ERROR CORRECTOR

### Forward Swing Errors and Their Corrections

*Too much muscular force*
> Relax the muscles of the shoulder and allow the pendulum swing to increase the velocity of the ball.

*Poor balance prior to, during, or after the release*
> Plant the sliding foot solidly and keep the center of gravity (hips) over the base of support (front foot). Do not drop the right shoulder or lean to the right or left. Keep your follow-through in the plane of the pendulum swing. Keep the ball of the rear foot planted.

Some obvious variables to consider on the release are:

1. The hand position on the ball.
2. When the thumb comes out of the ball in relation to the fingers.
3. The force of the fingers on the lift.
4. The squeezing action of the fingers.
5. Development of a consistent release from day to day.

People bowl for many years and fail to understand that with accuracy alone they will get only 30 to 40 percent strikes without an effective release. To develop a great release you must have all the basic fundamentals of the footwork and armswing. You must also have an understanding of lift and finger squeeze. Lift is imparted by keeping the fingers in the ball as long as you can in a straight continuous follow-through. Keep the fingers tense and have a firm wrist. The squeeze is imparted by a powerful flexing of the fingers. During the flexing of the fingers, the ball is released.

When releasing the ball, allow it to land six inches to a foot or more past the foul line. Work on developing a consistent release from day to day.

**The Follow-Through.** The follow-through is the final part of the pendulum swing. It is the upward arc that occurs after the release of the ball. If you have a good straight swing up to the point of release, just allow your arm to continue upward in a smooth flowing movement. Don't neglect your follow-through.

Once the release and follow-through are firmly established and the armswing is straight and consistent, if you still have errors, the source of the errors may be caused by improper choice of ball or ball fit.

**Coordinating the Timing.** The challenge in your footwork is to develop a sense of timing that will have your feet in the correct position in regard to the armswing. This may be accomplished by changing the footwork, the armswing, or both.

### The Three- and Five-Step Approaches

Since the four-step approach is the easiest approach to learn, it has been presented here in detail. In the five-step approach, one step is added at the beginning before the pushaway; therefore, the first step is

## THE SPORT EXPERIENCE

Practice the following activities to improve your release:

1. Place the hand in the "shake-hands" position. Forcefully flex the fingers. This will help with the squeeze. To practice the lift and squeeze, swing the arm and follow through, squeezing as the arm goes into the upswing after it has passed the front foot. "Snap" the middle two fingers into the palm of the hand.

2. Lift your ball from the floor using only the two middle fingers. Start with five lifts and build up to thirty.

3. Place the ball on the floor and put the middle and ring fingers in the finger holes. By the use of wrist and finger action practice the squeeze. At first, it may seem useless or silly, but continue to practice it and you will understand it. Your nervous system needs a little programming. Doing it will strengthen your release. Now insert your thumb and do the exercise, concentrating on getting your thumb out of the ball first. You may think your thumb won't come out, but it will.

4. Now apply the same exercises with the lifting or follow-through action on the carpet with a partner and then on the lanes. If your middle two fingers are in the palm of your hand after the release, you should be getting correct lift. You will notice the very powerful roll on the ball.

5. Now try lifting without squeezing. If you have developed the squeeze technique a little, you should see a tremendous difference in the ball roll. Make sure you are only lifting and not squeezing.

6. Practice the four steps with the release and use The Error Corrector checklist (p. 38) to analyze your errors.

# THE ERROR CORRECTOR

## Release Errors and Their Corrections

*Ball pulled to the left*
> Make sure the ball holes are the correct size. If the fit is correct, work on your timing to keep you from getting ahead of the ball.

*Ball pushed to the right*
> Correct your balance. Tense the muscles of the lower back. Plant the back foot on the approach.

*Ball released too soon*
> Check the ball holes for correct fit. Correct your timing. Your pushaway should be completed as the heel of your first step touches down. The ball should be moving into the forward swing as the third step is completed. A little more firmness in your fingers may help.

*Ball released too late*
> The holes in your ball may be too small.

*Ball not released in "shake-hands" position*
> Release the ball in the "shake-hands" position. Practice mentally and physically until you can do it.

*Loss of balance*
> Relax! Develop good timing. Make sure your footwork does not end too soon. Contract the muscles of the lower back. Keep your posture more erect. Keep the back foot on or closer to the approach.

## THE SPORT EXPERIENCE

Practice these exercises to develop a solid follow-through:

1. Without the ball, lift the arm smoothly upward until the elbow is face high. The arm should be slightly in front of the body, but some bowlers continue the follow-through until the elbow is beside the head. This is also acceptable.

2. Go through your normal approach and delivery. After the release, continue into the follow-through, and hold your position. Keep your eye on your target and maintain this balanced position until the ball contacts the pins.

3. Tape a towel or white piece of paper on the lane just past the foul line. The marks the ball will make as it makes contact will let you know where your ball is landing.

---

on the left foot for a right-handed bowler instead of on the right foot. The three-step approach is not an effective method of bowling and will not be included here.

## PRACTICE AND FEEDBACK

Develop a regular practice schedule. Practice! Practice! Practice! However, learn when to stop practicing and get away. Practicing when you are fatigued may be more detrimental than constructive.

Avoid competition until you have developed your skills. It is difficult to perfect your game when you are concentrating on beating someone.

Feedback is also necessary to improve your bowling. Bowling offers you almost immediate feedback. You can watch your mark and the ball and tell if you are accurate. You can tell if you hit your target and your pocket. You can determine how many pins a particular shot

# THE ERROR CORRECTOR

## Ball Errors

*Ball too heavy*
1. Causes shoulder to drop causing poor balance.
2. Causes a rushed approach and results in dropping the ball making a powerful release impossible.

*Ball too light*
1. May result in too much speed which causes too much deflection at the pins.
2. Results in a high swing affecting shoulder and body squareness to the target and timing.

*Too wide a span*
1. Places too much stress on the fingers and hand. You will tire too quickly.

*Too narrow a span*
1. Causes you to grip the ball just to hold it.
2. Causes poor control due to dropping the ball.
3. Causes difficulty with the release.
4. Yields no hook and less ball revolutions resulting in ineffective ball roll.

*Thumbhole too big*
1. Results in too much strain from gripping the ball.
2. Results in unnecessary strain destroying freedom in the swing.
3. Results in frequently dropping the ball, thus destroying the release. This is better than too small a hole because the inside of the hole can be taped to make it smaller. You can do this between frames if necessary.

*Thumbhole too small*
1. Makes it hard to get the thumb out of the ball.
2. Results in too short a time between the thumb and fingers leaving the ball, resulting in a poor release.

## THE SPORT EXPERIENCE

Contact a professional ball driller and get him to take the time to look at your approach, delivery, release, and ball track and determine the best individualized custom-fitted ball for your hand. It may be vital to helping you have a good release.

---

knocks over. Pay attention to the speed of your ball. An optimum ball speed is around 25 feet per second (2.4 seconds to reach the pins). If you bowl too slowly the ball will not have enough force to knock down the pins. However, if you bowl too fast, it may force the pins straight back, eliminating pin action. This is a built-in feedback system, but it does not provide information about your body movements. A friend or instructor, or video equipment, can offer such feedback.

Video equipment is readily available and tells the story better than any method available. To see yourself go through your smooth-flowing approach, take camera shots from various angles. These will allow you to identify your strengths as well as your weaknesses. Knowing your strengths is as important as knowing your weaknesses. Your strengths bring you success, not your weaknesses. Use the video shots to discover problems and then work to overcome the problems. Even for those of you who have video equipment available all the time, don't use it constantly. Identify strengths and weaknesses, then work with them a few days before you take another look.

Combine the video replay with good qualified instruction. You may be knowledgeable enough to spot errors, but you are also prejudiced. Allow someone you trust to analyze your game. He or she may see it differently than you do. You don't have to do what someone tells you, but you will have another point of view. Don't just listen to anyone who thinks he or she is better than you. Others may score higher than you do, but they may not have solid basics and may hurt your game rather than helping it. Be selective from whom you ask for help or to whom you look for advice. After the instructor gives you feedback, work with it for a while. After a period of practice, go back for more video analysis. Good luck with your skills!

# THE SPORT EXPERIENCE

Take some time now to practice your four-step approach and release. Have a friend check your bowling on the checklist below. (A = always, U = usually, S = sometimes, N = never)

                                              A    U    S    N

**Beginning stance:**

1. Weight of ball mostly in nondominant hand    ___ ___ ___ ___
2. Ball held about waist level in front of body    ___ ___ ___ ___
3. Bowling hand in ball in a "shake-hands" position    ___ ___ ___ ___
4. Weight balanced, feet even    ___ ___ ___ ___

**Approach steps and swing coordination:**

1. Ball pushed away with first step (push)    ___ ___ ___ ___
2. Ball down to right leg with second step (down)    ___ ___ ___ ___
3. Ball continues to backswing height on third step (back)    ___ ___ ___ ___
4. Ball forward with slide of left foot (forward)    ___ ___ ___ ___

**Approach-delivery form:**

1. Body faces straight ahead from first step to slide    ___ ___ ___ ___
2. Shoulders level and parallel to foul line ("square to target")    ___ ___ ___ ___
3. Body balanced throughout delivery    ___ ___ ___ ___
4. Straight pendulum swing and follow-through    ___ ___ ___ ___
5. Walk is in a straight line    ___ ___ ___ ___

**Ball release:**

1. Hand placed in ball in "shake-hands" position      ___ ___ ___ ___
2. Hand remains in "shake-hands" position throughout swing      ___ ___ ___ ___
3. Thumb comes out of ball first on release      ___ ___ ___ ___
4. Ball released at least six inches beyond foul line (reach out)      ___ ___ ___ ___

# 3

## Playing the Game

Now that you have mastered the skills of bowling, you are ready to play the game. Two important concepts you need to learn are how to keep score and strategies for knocking down pins.

## SCORING

| Name | 1 | 2 | 3 | 4 | 5 | 6 | 7 | 8 | 9 | 10 | Total |
|---|---|---|---|---|---|---|---|---|---|---|---|
|  | ⊠ | ⊠ | ⊠ | ⊠ | ⊠ | ⊠ | ⊠ | ⊠ | ⊠ | ⊠⊠⊠ | |
|  | 30 | 60 | 90 | 120 | 150 | 180 | 210 | 240 | 270 | 300 | |

First let's score a game to see how this is done. There are a few basic principles for each frame that will simplify the scoring process. These principles are outlined for you here.

### Basic Scoring Principles for Each Frame

*Open Frame* (less than ten pins knocked down):
   The score is the total pins knocked down with two balls in that frame.
*Spare* (ten pins knocked down with two balls in a frame):
   The score is 10 plus the pins knocked down on the next *ball* rolled. The maximum score for the frame is 20.
*Strike* (ten pins knocked down with the first ball of a frame):
   The score is 10 plus the pins knocked down with the next *two balls*. The maximum score for the frame is 30.

*Tenth Frame:*
A player with a strike or spare in the tenth frame rolls three balls.

As you bowl, make sure to write in the small boxes on your scoresheet the number of pins you knock down with each ball. The symbols on page 46 are used in scoring a game of bowling.

Now let's score a game. In the first frame you knock down three pins with the first ball and six of the remaining pins with the second ball. One pin is left standing. The frame will look like one of these examples depending on the scoresheet furnished to you.

In frame 2 you step over the foul line as you deliver the ball. A foul occurs when any part of the bowler's body touches anything on or beyond the foul line before the next delivery, even if it is not seen by a judge or umpire or recorded by a foul detecting device. *Deliberate* fouling results in a loss of score, with no further deliveries allowed in that frame. Even though you knocked down all ten pins, you receive no score for what would have been a strike. The pins are respotted (replaced) for your second ball. You knock them all down again to create a spare. You have now earned one bonus ball so you must wait to score until the *first ball* is rolled in the next frame.

In frame 3, you bowl a strike so the second ball is not needed. You can now score your spare by adding the 10 points from the bonus *ball* to the 10 points for your spare. A spare followed by a strike always counts 20 points. Add the 20 points to the score of the first frame for a cumulative score of 29. Your strike has now earned you two bonus *balls* so you must wait to score until you have bowled two more *balls*.

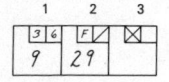

In frame 4, on your first ball you accidentally roll a ball in the gutter or channel alongside the lane so you score no points (even if the ball hops out and knocks some pins down). On your second ball you knock down nine pins. Since you failed to make a mark (a strike or a

*Playing the Game*

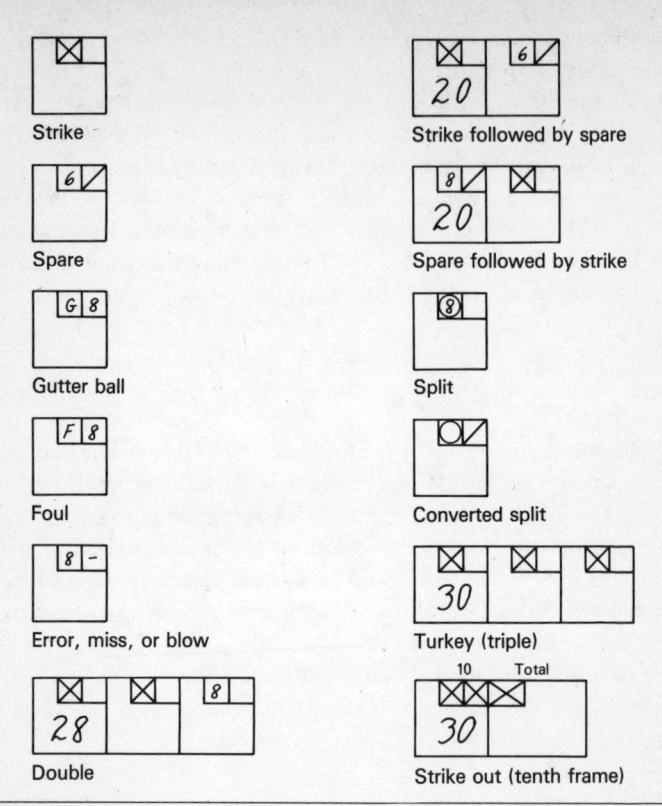

| Strike | Strike followed by spare |
| Spare | Spare followed by strike |
| Gutter ball | Split |
| Foul | Converted split |
| Error, miss, or blow | Turkey (triple) |
| Double | Strike out (tenth frame) |

**Scoring symbols**

spare) by knocking down all ten pins you have made an error. An error occurs when you fail to knock down all ten pins with two balls in a frame unless there is a split. It is marked with a dash in the second box above the 9. Go back to frame 1 as well and mark the error. (If no pins were knocked down the dash would stand alone in the second box.) This is also called an open frame. You can now score your strike in frame 3 by adding the 0 and 9 points from the *two balls* in frame 4 to the 10 points for the strike in frame 3. The 19 points are then added to the 29 points in frame 2 to obtain a running score of 48. The 9 points in frame 4, added to 48, results in a cumulative score of 57.

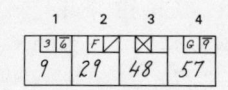

46    BOWLING

In frame 5 you roll another strike so you must wait to score this frame.

| 1 | 2 | 3 | 4 | 5 |
|---|---|---|---|---|
| 3 6 / 9 | F / 29 | X 48 | 6 7 / 57 | X |

In frame 6 you again roll a strike. Two strikes in a row are called a double. A double is worth from 20 to 29 points depending on the next ball rolled (which will be in frame 7).

| 1 | 2 | 3 | 4 | 5 | 6 |
|---|---|---|---|---|---|
| 3 6 / 9 | F / 29 | X 48 | 6 7 / 57 | X | X |

Frame 7: This time you knock down eight pins on the first ball, leaving a 5-6 split. A split is recorded by placing a circle in the box. You are lucky and knock down both pins on the second ball converting the split into a spare which is recorded in the usual way. You can now score frames 5 and 6 by adding the bonus *balls* to the 10 points for each strike. Frame 5 is worth 28 points (10 + 10 + 8), so the cumulative total is 85. Frame 6 is worth 20 points (10 + 8 + 2). A strike followed by a spare always equals 20 points. The running score is now 105.

| 1 | 2 | 3 | 4 | 5 | 6 | 7 |
|---|---|---|---|---|---|---|
| 3 6 / 9 | F / 29 | X 48 | 6 7 / 57 | X 85 | X 105 | ⑧ / |

In frame 8 you knock down eight pins leaving a 7-10 split. On the second ball you miss both pins. You might think at first that this is a miss or error. However, you can not have a miss when there is a split in the frame, so you leave the second box blank. (If you had knocked down one pin you would put a 1 in the box). You can now score the seventh and eighth frames. A spare plus the first ball bonus equals 18 (10 + 8), so the running score is 123 in the seventh frame. Eight plus 123 makes the cumulative score after eight frames 131.

| 1 | 2 | 3 | 4 | 5 | 6 | 7 | 8 |
|---|---|---|---|---|---|---|---|
| 3 6 / 9 | F / 29 | X 48 | 6 7 / 57 | X 85 | X 105 | ⑧ / 123 | ⑧ 131 |

In frame 9 you get five pins on the first ball and knock down three on the second ball, but your hand touches the lane on the other side

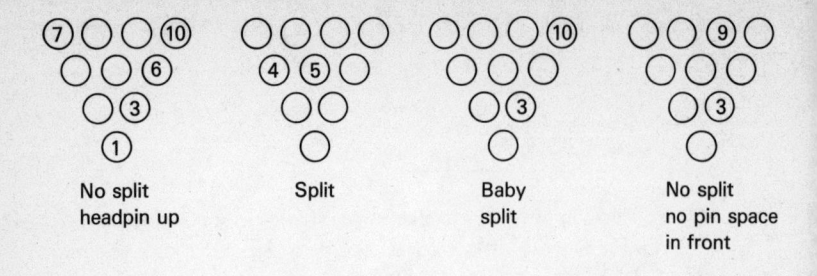

```
  ⑦○○⑩      ○○○○      ○○○⑩      ○○⑨○
  ○○⑥○      ④⑤○       ○○○       ○○○
  ○③        ○○        ○③        ○③
  ①         ○          ○          ○
  No split    Split      Baby       No split
  headpin up             split      no pin space
                                    in front
```

A split occurs when the headpin is down and one or more spaces (one or more pins down) exist between or in front of pins still standing, as seen from the front.

## Splits

of the foul line on your second delivery. Your score in the ninth frame is 136 (131 + 5).

| 1 | 2 | 3 | 4 | 5 | 6 | 7 | 8 | 9 |
|---|---|---|---|---|---|---|---|---|
| 3 / | F / | X | 0 9 | X | X | 8 / | 8 / | 5 F |
| 9 | 29 | 48 | 57 | 85 | 105 | 123 | 131 | 136 |

Let's take a break from scoring to review the rules governing pinfall.

*Legal pinfall*

1. Pins rebounding from the side partition, rear cushion, or sweep bar *at rest*, and downing pins.

2. If pins are set incorrectly, but all are there:
   a. Accept resulting pinfall *or*
   b. Ask for pins to be respotted *before* bowling

*Illegal pinfall* (ball counts as ball rolled, pins downed don't count—replace those pins for the next ball)

1. Pins knocked down by a ball that leaves the lane or hits dead wood first.

2. Ball rebounds from rear cushion and downs pins.

3. Pins downed by the pinsetter after the first ball.

4. Foul—any part of the bowler's body goes beyond the foul line and touches any part of the lane equipment or building.

*Dead ball pinfall* (pins are respotted and ball is rebowled)

1. Pin missing from setup.

2. Bowling out of turn or on the wrong lane (if discovered before another player has bowled; if not, continue as is except in singles match play, when lanes are corrected for further play).

3. Obstruction of ball, or pins moved or knocked down before contact.

4. Physical interference with the bowler during delivery (bowler may accept pinfall or rebowl immediately).

In the tenth frame several possible situations can occur. If you have an open frame the game is over with no bonus balls as shown here:

| 1 | 2 | 3 | 4 | 5 | 6 | 7 | 8 | 9 | 10 | Total |
|---|---|---|---|---|---|---|---|---|---|---|
| 3\|6 | F\|/ | ⊠ | 6\|3 | ⊠ | ⊠ | 8\|/ | 8 | 5\|F | 7\|2 | |
| 9 | 29 | 48 | 57 | 85 | 105 | 123 | 131 | 136 | 145 | 145 |

However, if you roll a strike or a spare, you must roll your bonus ball or balls in order to score the frame as in the following examples (136 + 10 + 10):

| 1 | 2 | 3 | 4 | 5 | 6 | 7 | 8 | 9 | 10 | Total |
|---|---|---|---|---|---|---|---|---|---|---|
| 3\|6 | F\|/ | ⊠ | 6\|3 | ⊠ | ⊠ | 8\|/ | 8 | 5\|F | 7\|⊠ | |
| 9 | 29 | 48 | 57 | 85 | 105 | 123 | 131 | 136 | 156 | 156 |

| 1 | 2 | 3 | 4 | 5 | 6 | 7 | 8 | 9 | 10 | Total |
|---|---|---|---|---|---|---|---|---|---|---|
| 3\|6 | F\|/ | ⊠ | 6\|3 | ⊠ | ⊠ | 8\|/ | 8 | 5\|F | ⊠\|8 | |
| 9 | 29 | 48 | 57 | 85 | 105 | 123 | 131 | 136 | 156 | 156 |

When a spare or strike is made with the *bonus* balls in the tenth frame it is dead and no more balls are rolled. Note that the final score is carried over into the totals column. Later this column will be used to keep a cumulative score for your team. A strike out in the tenth frame looks like this and is worth 30 points (10 + 10 + 10):

| 1 | 2 | 3 | 4 | 5 | 6 | 7 | 8 | 9 | 10 | Total |
|---|---|---|---|---|---|---|---|---|---|---|
| 3\|6 | F\|/ | ⊠ | 6\|3 | ⊠ | ⊠ | 8\|/ | 8 | 5\|F | ⊠⊠⊠ | |
| 9 | 29 | 48 | 57 | 85 | 105 | 123 | 131 | 136 | 166 | 166 |

Some bowlers like to black in spares and strikes as in the following example:

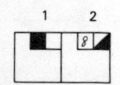

| 1 | 2 |
|---|---|
| ■ | 8\|/ |

Playing the Game

## THE SPORT EXPERIENCE

Now try your hand at scoring a game. First look at the bowling scores for Heidi and Chris:

**Scoring Practice Sheet for Heidi**

| Frame | First Ball | Second Ball | Circumstances |
|---|---|---|---|
| 1 | 9 | 0 | |
| 2 | 10 | – | |
| 3 | 8 | 2 | |
| 4 | 10 | – | |
| 5 | 9 | 1 | foul on second ball |
| 6 | 7 | 3 | 4-6-10 split |
| 7 | 4 | 6 | |
| 8 | 8 | 0 | big four split |
| 9 | 10 | – | |
| 10 | 10 | 8 | 2 on third ball |

**Scoring Practice Sheet for Chris**

| Frame | First Ball | Second Ball | Circumstances |
|---|---|---|---|
| 1 | 7 | 2 | |
| 2 | 10 | – | |
| 3 | 10 | – | |
| 4 | 10 | – | |
| 5 | 6 | 2 | 4-6-7-9 split |
| 6 | 10 | – | |
| 7 | 10 | – | |
| 8 | 3 | 7 | |
| 9 | 10 | 6 | foul on first ball |
| 10 | 10 | 10 | 6 on third ball |

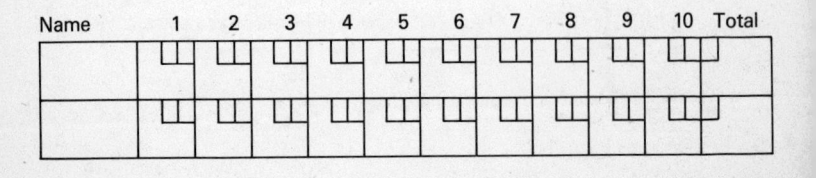

| Name | 1 | 2 | 3 | 4 | 5 | 6 | 7 | 8 | 9 | 10 | Total |
|---|---|---|---|---|---|---|---|---|---|---|---|
| | | | | | | | | | | | |
| | | | | | | | | | | | |

BOWLING

1. Mark the correct symbols and score each line of bowling on the scoring practice sheet (page 50). Compare your answers with those in Appendix D. Review any areas on which you had difficulty.

2. Go to a bowling center that has automatic scoring. Score your games on the practice sheet and compare your answers with those provided.

3. Go to a bowling center during league or tournament bowling. Score the players' games and compare your scores with those on the telescores.

4. Teach a friend how to score.

## AIMING METHODS

A perfect strike occurs when the ball moves diagonally from the right side of the lane into the 1-3 pocket for a right-handed bowler (or from the left side of the lane into the 1-2 pocket for a left-hander). The ball should hit the right half of the headpin and the left third of the 3 pin. The 1 pin knocks down the 2, 4, and 7 pins like dominoes. The 3 pin downs the 6 and 10 pins. The ball continues into the 5 and 9 pins and

**The strike pocket**

Playing the Game 51

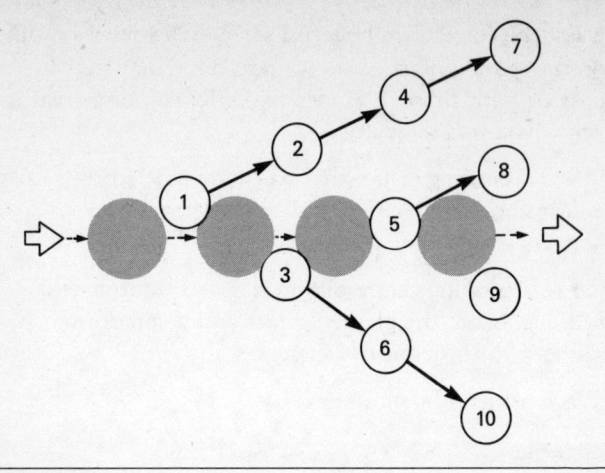

**The strike ball**

the 8 pin is knocked down by the 5 pin. If the ball hits too high on the headpin, a split occurs. Hitting too much on the 3 pin results in a center or kingpin leave.

Developing a solid method of aiming will improve your accuracy in hitting the pocket. Without accuracy it is difficult to get strikes or convert spares. There are three methods of aiming—pin bowling, spot bowling, and line bowling.

Keep in mind that you must have a consistent and smooth approach and delivery to most effectively utilize these principles. If your delivery is inconsistent, you will not know if your errors are due to the poor use of strategies or to your inconsistency.

## *Pin Bowling*

Pin bowling is a method of aiming in which the bowler aims only at the pins. It is the least effective method and is used primarily by beginners. Stop pin bowling! Learn to spot bowl. After you learn to spot bowl, try the line bowling method.

## *Spot Bowling*

Spot bowling is the most frequently used method of aiming. The name refers to the fact that the bowler is aiming for a particular spot on the lane and trying to roll the ball over that spot. The most frequently

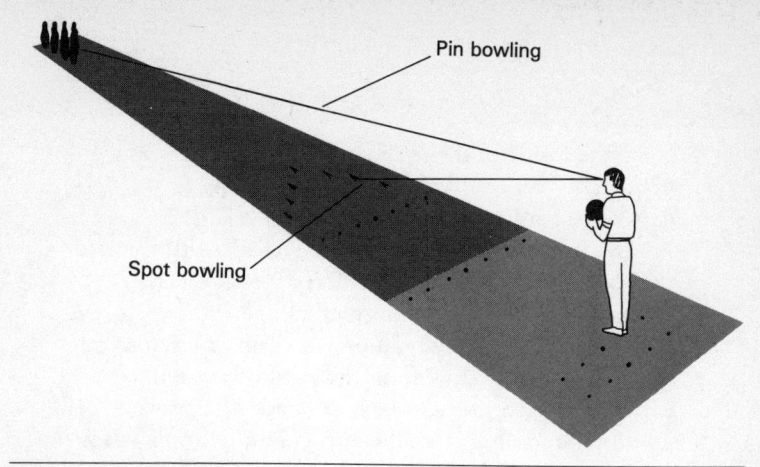

**Pin and spot bowling**

used spots are the arrows imbedded in the lanes approximately fifteen feet past the foul line. Dots about seven feet past the foul line are sometimes used. You could use any spot on the lane that is easily seen. The main reason for using the dots and arrows is that they are on all lanes and they are a much closer target than the pins, which are sixty feet away. For every one inch (approximately one board) change near the spots, the ball moves approximately three inches at the pins.

## Line Bowling

This is an advanced method of spot bowling. Identify a line from the foul line to the pins on which the ball should roll. This line will cross many spots along the line including a spot or board at the foul line, a dot, and an arrow or a board between the arrows. It terminates in the pocket between the pins you desire to hit.

# PATTERNS OF BALL ROLL

There are at least four patterns of ball roll—the straight ball, the backup, the curve, and the hook. The straight ball is the least effective and the hook ball is the most effective in getting a high percentage of strikes.

*Playing the Game*

# THE SPORT EXPERIENCE

1. Place the inside of the *left* foot on board fifteen on the approach. You can find this board by going to the right gutter or channel and counting fifteen boards to the left. An easier method is to familiarize yourself with the location of the dots after you position yourself on the fifteenth board. Now walk to the foul line and look at the dots and arrows. Decide on one of them to use for your spot (the second arrow from the right or the tenth board if you are aiming for a strike). Go back and get your ball, position yourself on the fifteenth board, and roll at your spot. If your ball hits the 1-3 pocket, stay there and repeat the shot. If your ball goes too far to the right, move your feet to the right on your next strike shot. Keep moving until you hit the pocket. Once you hit the pocket, stay there and practice rolling the ball over your spot. See if you hit the pocket when you hit the spot. You may choose the first or third arrows. For this exercise, the choice of target doesn't matter, just practice rolling the ball over your spot and into the pocket.

2. This is a balance and concentration exercise related to spot bowling. Roll your ball over the target and keep your eyes on the spot until the ball contacts the pins. If you lose your balance, your concentration on your spot will be reduced. It is also more difficult to determine whether you hit or missed your target. Keep your eyes on your spot from the beginning of your approach until the ball contacts the pins. Practice this exercise regularly and your concentration and balance will improve. Both are very important to effective spot bowling.

3. This exercise is for area spot bowling. This will require an understanding proprietor. Tape some soft material to to the first and second arrows and attempt to roll your ball between the two arrows without hitting the taped material. Attempting to hit one board is difficult and results in increased tension, while area bowling allows

the bowler to relax. The relaxed effort and attitude help the bowler to be more accurate.

4. Place a sheet in front of the pins and bowl using the spots to aim, relying on the pin indicator to tell you what pins are standing.

# THE SPORT EXPERIENCE

1. Identify your stance position. Roll the ball using the spot bowling method. Once you get in the pocket, pick a spot closer than the arrows. Now watch the ball roll over both spots. After you become skilled at two spots, pick one thirty to forty feet down the lane and hit all three spots as the ball rolls toward your strike. You really have four spots, which include the three on the lane and the pocket. See if you can hit your release point, spot one, spot two, spot three, the pocket, and get a strike. Mastery of this exercise will greatly improve your accuracy and scores.

2. Keep your eyes on your first spot. After the ball rolls over the first spot, watch the ball roll over each spot in turn, hit the pocket, and get your strike. Concentrate on each of the spots as the ball rolls over them. This is designed so that you will concentrate on the ball as it rolls down the lane. Determine what about line bowling creates your success and what creates your failure at striking.

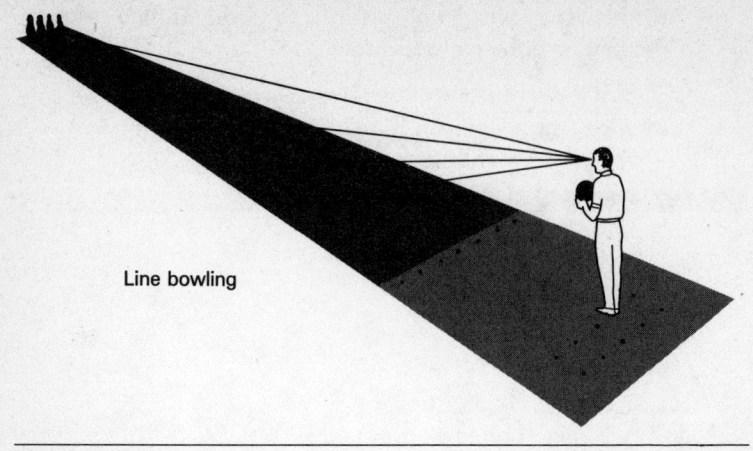

**Line bowling**

## *The Straight Ball*

The straight ball is released with the thumb at 12 o'clock. The ball rolls in a straight line from the point of release to the pins. You could roll it directly down the 17 board and hit the 1-3 pocket. However, the angle would be poor and the ball would deflect out of the pocket, so it is better to angle it across the lane from the right side. Because the straight ball hits too much of the 3 pin and too little of the 5 pin, it results in few strikes and many splits. If you plan to do more than a limited amount of bowling, learn to deliver a hook ball. If you insist on using the straight ball, move over to the first arrow and bowl a diagonal right to left line to the pocket. Maintain good ball speed and hit more of the headpin than the 3 pin. The straight ball is good for making spares, but don't expect a very high average. If you want strikes and a high average, learn the hook ball delivery.

## *The Backup Ball*

The backup ball is rolled by twisting the hand and wrist clockwise during the release so that the thumb comes out of the ball at 1 o'clock. The ball goes directly down the lane until it is ten to twenty feet from the pins and breaks sharply to the right. The backup ball does not

**Straight ball**     **Backup ball**     **Curve ball**     **Hook ball**

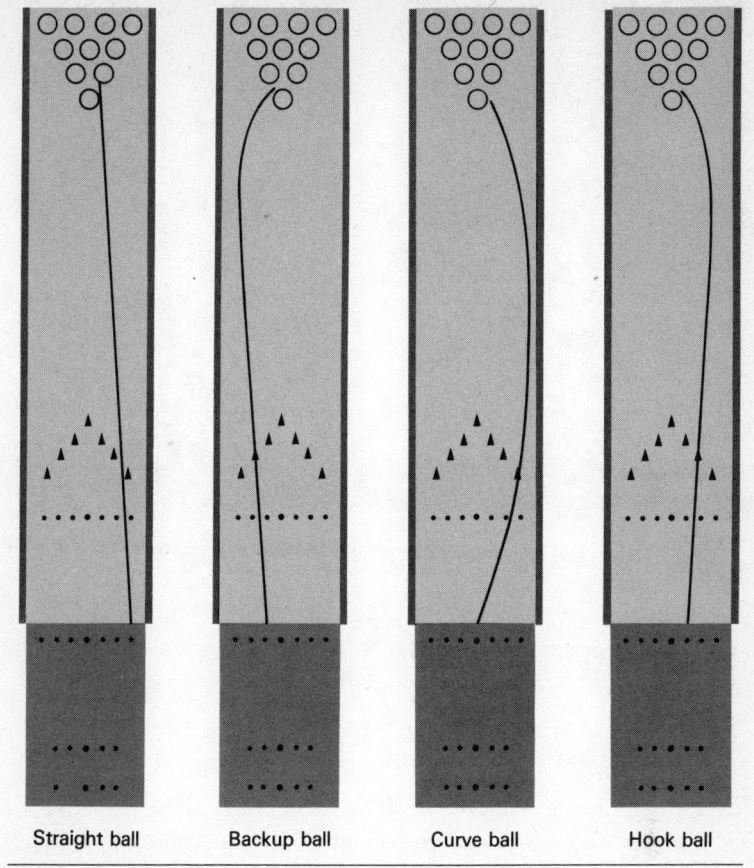

**Patterns of ball roll**

have the mechanical advantage of a hook ball. From a palm forward position, it is weak and unnatural to move the right hand in a clockwise direction. Since a weak wrist may cause a backup ball, work on exercises to strengthen the wrist or wear a wristband.

## *The Curve Ball*

The curve ball is rolled with an inward rotation of the wrist, so that the thumb leaves the ball at 9 or 10 o'clock. The curve ball differs from the hook ball in that it moves more slowly and across more boards

Straight ball                    Hook ball

**Release positions for ball roll**

making it harder to control accuracy. It also reduces the power at the pins. It is better to learn the hook ball.

### The Hook Ball

High average bowlers use the hook ball. It is rolled with the hand in a "shake-hands" position, with the thumb at 10 o'clock and a firm wrist. The ball goes directly down the lane until it is ten to twenty feet from the pins and then breaks sharply toward the pins. Releasing the hook ball correctly will give you skid, roll, and hook in the proper amounts. These are all necessary for explosive action at the pins, which results in an abundance of strikes.

## ANGLE ADJUSTMENTS FOR STRIKES AND SPARES

The lane is divided into boards. There are usually 39 boards on a lane. There are 19 boards to the left and 19 boards to the right of center, so counting from the left or right, the center or 20 board will be the

**Boards and arrows on approach and rangefinder**

*(Courtesy of Brunswick Division)*

fourth arrow. It is the arrow closest to the headpin. These boards are important for angle adjustments as well as for aiming. The arrows are five boards apart. The first arrow is the 5 board, the second is the 10 board, etc. The arrows and dots help simplify angle adjustments. You don't have to count each board on every shot. Just learn to use the markings on the lane.

## *Strikes*

Position yourself four and one-half steps from the foul line and fifteen boards from the gutter on your dominant-hand side. Use the dots on the approach to help you remember where your stance is each time. This will also make it easier to make adjustments for lane conditions and spare conversions. Start from the same position on the approach for each strike. The position will change for different lanes and conditions, but should never change from shot to shot.

Angle adjustments for strikes are made by moving your feet or your target. Sometimes the adjustments may require you to move both your feet and your target. The feet are adjusted by moving left or right

# THE SPORT EXPERIENCE

Practice the exercises for the release as explained in Chapter 2. Then check yourself or have a partner check to see if the ball is getting the correct action. Use the following checklist. Mark Y (yes) or N (no) for each trial.

### Trials

1 2 3 4 5 6 7 8 9 10 11 12

1. Hand starts in the "shake-hands" position

2. Hand position is the same throughout the swing

3. On release—LIFT

4. Wrist rigid on release

5. Follow-through straight up

6. Ball skids

7. Ball hooks

---

on the approach prior to your delivery. The target changes are also left or right. If the second arrow is your target, a right change would be the 9 to 1 boards. A left change would be the 11 board or higher (farther left). Remember that a one-inch change equals approximately three inches at the pins.

## *Spares*

To make proper adjustments for spares, you should establish three positions. The first, which you have already practiced is the strike position. The second is the 10-pin shot and the third is the 7-pin shot. The strike position will cover spare shots involving the headpin and the 5 pin. The 10-pin position will cover spares on the right side of the

Moving feet          Moving target

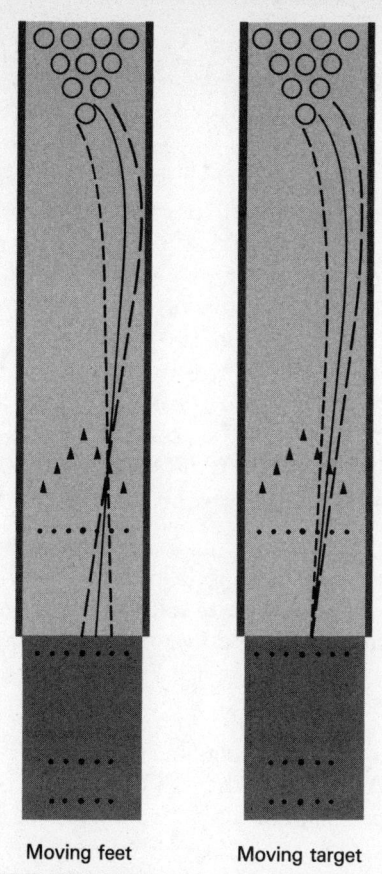

**Angle adjustments for strikes**

headpin such as the 3, 6, 9, and 10 pins. The stance for the 10-pin shot is on the extreme left side of the lane. The third arrow from the right is a good 10-pin target. The 7-pin position will cover spares on the left side such as the 2, 4, 7 and 8 pins. The stance for the 7-pin shot is nine boards right of your strike position, with the target being your strike spot; or your stance is the strike stance and your target is six or seven boards to the left of your strike target. After these positions are established you need to understand two methods for adjusting to convert spares. They are the 3-6-9 method, in which you move your feet, and the 2-4-6- method, in which you move your target.

*Playing the Game*

# THE SPORT EXPERIENCE

1. Start by positioning your feet on the approach and remember where you are located. Make your approach and delivery. Roll the ball over the second arrow and hit the pocket and get a strike. If your ball went to the right of your target and you started with the inside of your left foot on the 15 board, move right to the 14 or smaller board. To speed things up, use this system: If you hit the 10 pin, move six boards to the right to the 9 board and hit the second arrow. If everything else remained constant, you should be in the pocket. If you hit the 6 pin, move four boards to the right, or the 3 pin, two boards to the right. If you are between pins, move one, three, or five boards.

2. This exercise is designed to help you understand different lines to the pocket. Practice rolling the ball along the gutter (boards 1 to 3) and over each arrow to see the different lines created by changes in the target.

3. If your lane operator will allow it, practice bowling your strike ball between the Big Four (4-6-7-10 pins) without knocking down any of the pins (Shunk, Carol, *Bowling*, third edition, San Francisco: Saunders College Publishing, 1983, p. 83)

4. If your lane operator will do so, set up only the 1, 2 and 3 pins and take turns knocking them down. Score the number of pins knocked down on each ball. The first player to reach twenty points wins.

5. Use the bowling practice sheet (page 63) to analyze your strike ball. Make changes as needed to hit the pocket consistently.

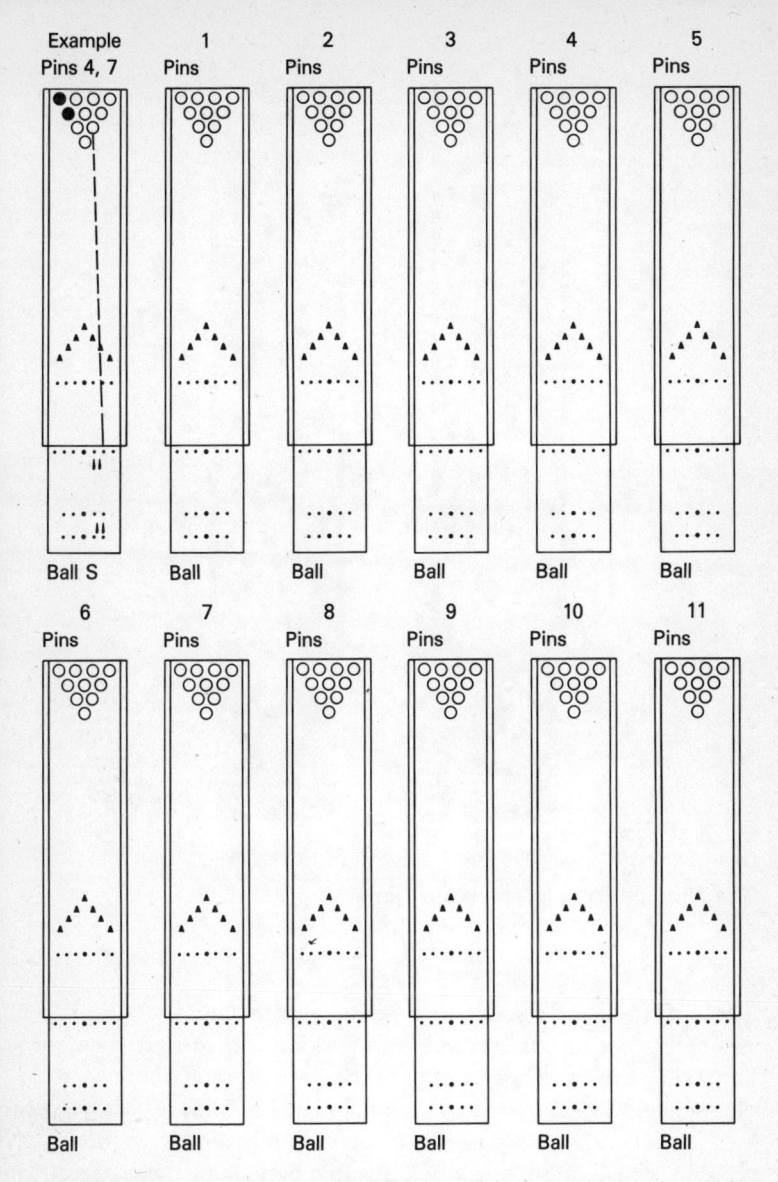

| Example<br>Pins 4, 7 | 1<br>Pins | 2<br>Pins | 3<br>Pins | 4<br>Pins | 5<br>Pins |
|---|---|---|---|---|---|
| Ball S | Ball | Ball | Ball | Ball | Ball |

| 6<br>Pins | 7<br>Pins | 8<br>Pins | 9<br>Pins | 10<br>Pins | 11<br>Pins |
|---|---|---|---|---|---|
| Ball | Ball | Ball | Ball | Ball | Ball |

On each diagram record the type of ball (hook, straight, curve, back-up); mark feet ( ıı ) in positions at start and release; draw path of ball; blacken pins left and record them also on the chart for spot bowling spares; mark X over all if strike. See example.

## Spot-bowling—Strikes

*Playing the Game*

7-pin position        10-pin position

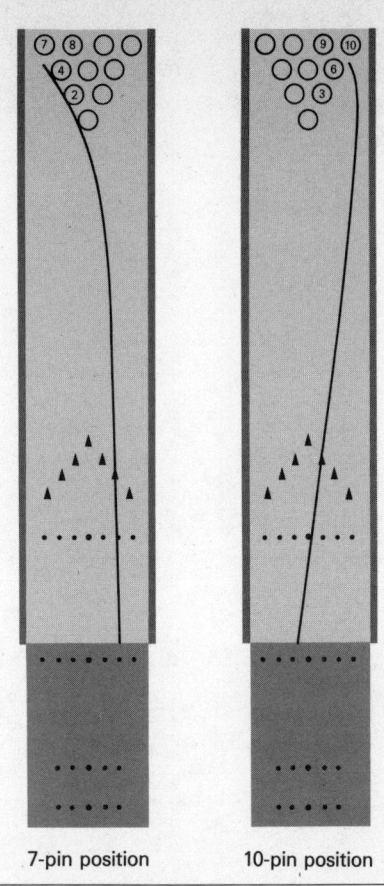

**The 7-pin and 10-pin spare positions**

***3-6-9 Method.*** The 3-6-9 method involves moving your feet. Right side spares are shot from the 10-pin position. To convert the 6 pin, move your feet three boards right of the 10-pin spot. To convert the 3 pin, move six boards to the right, and for the 1 pin, move nine boards.

The 2, 4, 7, and 8 pins can be picked up by adjusting the strike position. The 2 or 8 pin can be converted by moving three boards to the right of the strike position. The 4 and 7 pins are covered by moving six and nine boards to the right. To cover spares with more than one pin, determine if the ball or pins are to do the work and adjust according to your decision. When pins are behind each other at a diagonal, such as in a 2-4-7 leave, the ball could take all three pins down or the ball could take out the 2. The 2 could take out the 4 and the 4 could trip the 7. However, it is best to use the ball to hit as many pins as possible. Choose the position which places the ball closest to the center of the leave. The 3-10 split could be made by deflecting the 3 pin into the 10 pin, but it is easier to hit both pins with the ball.

**2-4-6 Method.** The 2-4-6 method involves moving your target. For right-side spares, shoot the 10 pin from the 10-pin position. Move the target two boards left of the 10-pin target for the 6 pin. If the third ar-

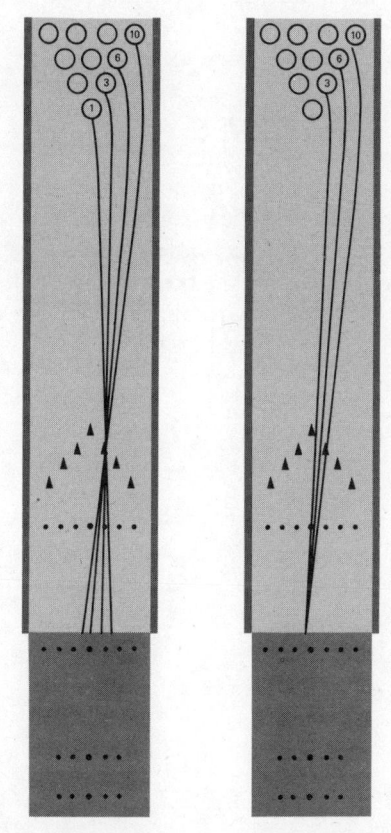

The 3-6-9 method (feet move)   The 2-4-6 method (target moves)

**Methods of spare conversions**

row (15 board) is the 10-pin target, the 17 board would be the 6-pin target. For the 3 pin, move the target to the 19 board or four boards to the left. Shoot the left side by moving two boards to the left of the strike target for the 2 pin, four boards to the left for the 4 pin, and six boards to the left for the 7 pin.

Try both methods to determine which works best for you. You may find that the 3-6-9 becomes a 3-6-7 or a 4-6-8. The 2-4-6 may be a 2-4-7 or some other combination. Using the 2-4-6 or 3-6-9 will make it much easier and faster to determine where to stand or which target to use when preparing to convert your spares. The lane conditions or your style of bowling may contribute to differences in the 2-4-6 and 3-6-9 systems, but the system you choose will give you a guide to start from. Develop a system that you understand and that helps you convert your spares.

## *ADVANCED STRATEGIES*

As a beginning bowler, you should practice on the same lane every time you bowl, if possible. After you have had some experience, go to a different bowling center and try bowling on different lanes. When you do this you will discover that bowling lanes differ considerably from one another. Strategies for reading and adjusting to these varying lane conditions are presented in Chapter 5.

# THE SPORT EXPERIENCE

Establish the stance and target for your strike, 7-pin, and 10-pin positions. Then experiment with the 3-6-9 and 2-4-6 methods of aiming and choose the one that works for your spare shooting.

1. Practice your strike position to pick up the 1 and 5 pins. Write down your strike target arrow or board and your stance position.

2. Move to the extreme left side of the lane (extreme right if left-handed) and bowl over the third arrow from the gutter. Your ball should hit the 10 pin. If it does not, move your target one or more boards to the left or right until your ball consistently knocks down the 10 pin. Write down your stance and target positions.

3. Using the stance for your strike ball, aim six or seven boards to the left of your strike target *or* move nine boards to the right of your strike stance and aim at your strike target. Move your target or stance one board at a time until your ball consistently knocks down the 7 pin. Write down your stance and target positions.

4. Experiment with the 3-6-9 method of picking up spares by starting at the 10-pin position and moving your feet three boards to the right of the 10-pin spot for each pin (i.e., 6 pin = 3 boards right, 3 pin = 6 boards, 1 pin = 9 boards). Adjust your feet one board at a time until you are consistent. Try the same method for left-side spares, starting with the 7-pin position. Write down your target and stance positions for each pin.

5. Experiment with the 2-4-6 method of picking up spares by starting at the 10-pin position and moving your target two boards to the left of the 10-pin target for each pin (i.e., 6 pin = 2 boards, 3 pin = 4 boards, 1 pin = 6 boards). Try the same method for left-side spares, starting with the 7-pin position. Write down your target and stance positions for each pin.

6. Reverse bowling. Knock down all ten pins on the first ball, then nine pins only on two rolls, then eight pins on two rolls, etc. Score 10 points for each frame bowled correctly (i.e., exact number of pins downed—no more nor less) and 0 for each incorrect frame.

7. Accuracy bowling game. The object of this game is to score 100 points. Score 10 for each frame correctly bowled as prescribed. Score 0 for only partially correct frames. You earn 10 or 0 for each frame.

Frame 1   Roll a strike.
Frame 2   Knock down a minimum of eight pins with the first ball.
Frame 3   Leave only the 4 and 7 pins after two balls.
Frame 4   Roll a spare.
Frame 5   Leave the 1-2-3-5 pins standing after two balls.
Frame 6   Leave only the headpin standing after two balls.
Frame 7   Knock down only the 7 and 10 pins with two balls.
Frame 8   Knock down no more than five pins with both balls (no gutter balls).
Frame 9   Leave only the 7 and 10 pins standing after two balls.
Frame 10  Leave only three pins standing after two balls.

8. Strikes and pins. Each player has two rolls in each frame. Score two points for strikes and five points for knocking down the 7 or 10 pin (without knocking down neighboring pins). The player with the highest score wins.

9. 7-10 pin bowling. Knock down the 7 pin with the first ball and the 10 pin with the second ball. Score one point for each pin knocked down. A perfect game is twenty points. The player with the highest score wins (Shunk, Carol, *Bowling*, third edition. San Francisco: Saunders College Publishing, 1983, p. 84).

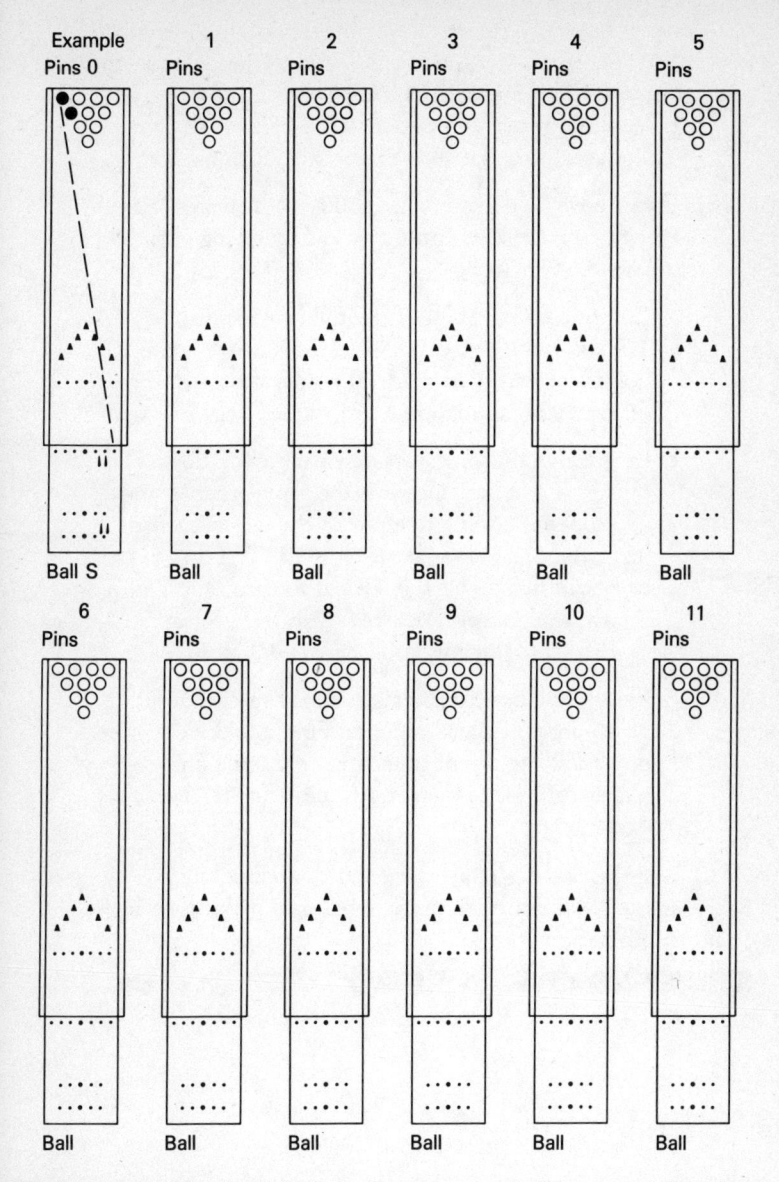

| Example | 1 | 2 | 3 | 4 | 5 |
|---|---|---|---|---|---|
| Pins 0 | Pins | Pins | Pins | Pins | Pins |
| Ball S | Ball | Ball | Ball | Ball | Ball |

| 6 | 7 | 8 | 9 | 10 | 11 |
|---|---|---|---|---|---|
| Pins | Pins | Pins | Pins | Pins | Pins |
| Ball | Ball | Ball | Ball | Ball | Ball |

Blacken pins left after first ball. Then record the type of ball (hook, straight, curve, back-up); mark feet ( ιι ) in positions at start and release; draw path of ball; mark pins left after second ball. See example.

## Spot-bowling—Spares

Playing the Game

10. Least pins. Try to knock down as few pins as possible with each ball (no gutter balls). For example, knocking down the 7 pin and then rolling the ball through its hole would result in a perfect score of 1 for that frame. The player with the *lowest* score wins (Shunk, p. 83).

11. If you bowl in a center that will allow you to set up specific pin combinations, play the following games with a partner or group:

    a. Roll one ball at each of the following splits: 2-7, 3-10, 4-5, 5-6, 5-10, 5-7, 6-7, 4-10, 4-7-10, 2-7-8. Score 10 points for each one made; 0 points if missed. The player with the highest score wins.

    b. Progressive bowling, version one. Knock down the pins in order, starting with the 1 pin; then 1 and 2; 1, 2, 3; etc., adding one pin to the set-up each time until you are rolling at all ten pins. The first player to bowl a strike wins. (Kidwell, Kathro, and Paul Smith, Jr., *Bowling Analyzed*. Dubuque, Iowa: Wm. C. Brown Company Publishers, 1960, p. 81.)

    c. Progressive bowling, version two. Knock down the pins, one at a time, in order. First knock down the 1 pin, then the 2 pin, then the 3 pin, etc. The first player to knock down the 10 pin wins (Kidwell, p. 81).

12. Use the practice chart (page 69) to analyze your spares. Make corrections as needed to pick up each pin combination.

# 4
# League and Tournament Play

Now that you have learned some of the skills and strategies of bowling, you are ready to enter the competitive world of bowling. In this chapter we will introduce you to the various types of leagues and tournaments, along with the concepts you will need to get started.

Enter the competitive situation slowly. Start by competing with yourself. Bowl a complete game of ten frames without concern for the score. Your goal is to leave no pins standing. Attempt to get a strike or spare in each frame. If you are unable to get through ten frames, see how many you can do without an open frame. If you miss, accept it and try again. When you reach your goal, reward yourself. You know the things that would be a reward for you. Competitive bowlers are rewarded when they accomplish their objectives. Practice rewarding yourself for your successes. It will prepare you for the real world of bowling.

If you have the self-control, don't score a game until you can get ten frames in a row without an open frame. Can you accept this challenge? You will have to have wise practice sessions if you ever want to keep score. Conquer this challenge and you will be pleased when you do finally keep score.

Next, get a bowling partner and challenge him or her to a game in which winning is determined by the one who gets the most marks in the game. Don't keep score. Concentrate on getting marks. Take your partner for a treat and relax after you compete. Competing should improve the quality of your life. If it doesn't, don't compete. Competition often puts a fine edge on your skills.

The next time you compete, let the loser pay for the treat. A small prize sometimes motivates people to do their best. Even a small amount of pressure makes some people do worse. You will have to learn to deal with pressure to succeed in competitive bowling. Now, bowl for a score. As you improve your average, you will leave many bowlers behind. If you can get a high percentage of strikes or spares each game, you are ahead of most bowlers. People usually develop their skills to socialize or to compete. Spend a lot of time in a bowling center and you will become aware that the social structure is centered around competition. This competition is in the form of pot bowling, leagues, and tournaments. Each form of competitive bowling offers a prize to the winner.

In pot bowling, each bowler puts a predetermined amount of money in the prize fund and the winner or winners take the money. This happens after each game or series of games. Tournaments use the same principle. An entry fee is paid before entering the tournament. Additional money or sponsor's money is added to the prize fund. The bowlers compete by rolling a predetermined number of games. There may be as many as twenty-four or forty-eight money winners in a large tournament. Leagues also have prize money, but the money is distributed at the end of the bowling season.

## *BOWLING LEAGUES*

A league is a group of teams or individuals who compete according to a prearranged schedule, usually round robin, in which every team plays every other team. There are men's leagues, women's leagues, mixed leagues (in which men and women compete, usually on the same teams), junior leagues, mixed adult-junior leagues, singles' leagues (one-person teams) and seniors' leagues (over age 55). Closed leagues are limited to members of a particular organization. In commercial leagues, the teams are sponsored by employers, who pay all fees. Each of these leagues can be open or scratch leagues, classified leagues, or handicap leagues.

In an open or scratch league, actual scores decide the winners of games. These leagues are usually limited to bowlers with very high averages.

In a classified league, there are different divisions based on averages. For example, if your average is 150, you would enter the division for bowlers who have averages near 150.

In a handicap league, a handicap or equalizer is added to give each bowler or team an equal chance to win. The handicap is based on the bowler's average.

## Averages

Your bowling average is essential to entry in a league or tournament. It is calculated by dividing the total of all game scores (without handicaps) by the number of games bowled.

$$\text{Average} = \frac{\text{Total scores of all games}}{\text{Number of games bowled}}$$

Bowlers who have averages for twenty-one games or more from the previous season use those averages for the first twelve to eighteen games of league play. Then new averages are calculated from the scores of the current season. Each week after bowling, the three games are added to those already bowled and a new average calculated. Fractions are always dropped. For beginning bowlers, who have no previous averages, some leagues establish a figure such as 120 or 140 which can be used for the first three games until an average can be calculated. Other leagues wait until after the first three games and then calculate an average and handicap for use with those three games and the next three games. The league secretary's book might show the following for one bowler:

| Date | Game 1 | Game 2 | Game 3 | Total | Accum. | Aver. |
|------|--------|--------|--------|-------|--------|-------|
| 3/15 | 145    | 152    | 140    | 437   | 437    | 145   |
| 3/22 | 165    | 140    | 135    | 440   | 877    | 146   |
| 3/29 | 172    | 146    | 121    | 439   | 1316   | 146   |

The scores 145, 152, and 140 are totaled (437) and divided by three games to get an average of 145. Note that the fraction was dropped. The second week the scores 165, 140, and 135 are added to the total from last week (437) to get 877, which is divided by six games to get 146. When a bowler bowls in more than one league, a composite average of games from both leagues or the highest average from all of the leagues may be required for entry in tournaments or other leagues.

A team average is the sum of the averages of its members. For example, the average for the following team is 621:

| Sue   | 141 |
| John  | 172 |
| Miguel| 169 |
| Mary  | 139 |
| Total | 621 |

Some leagues use computer programs to calculate bowlers' averages each week.

## Handicaps

A handicap is used to equalize competition, giving all bowlers an equal chance to win. It is added to the score of an individual or team. All handicaps are based on a scratch figure chosen by the league. The scratch figure is an arbitrary figure higher than the average of the best bowler in the league. Men's leagues often use a scratch figure of 200, while women's leagues might use 180.

The bowler's average is subtracted from the scratch figure and then a percentage of that difference (60–95%) is used as a handicap. The percentage varies from league to league. The higher the percentage, the greater chance a lower average bowler has of beating a higher average bowler. In fact, an ABC study showed that handicap percentages of 80 percent or less *never* allow lower-average teams to win league championships (*1984–85 ABC Constitution, Specifications & Rules and Suggested League Rules*, p. 102).

The handicap is added to the total pin score to obtain the bowler's game score. Handicaps change from week to week as new scores are averaged in.

A team handicap can be determined in one of two ways—the individual method or the team method. Each league decides on the type of handicap to be used.

In the individual method, the *handicaps* of all bowlers on a team are added together to get the team handicap. The individual method is

**Figuring Handicaps**

| Scratch figure   | 200   |                |
| Bowler's average | − 160 |                |
| Difference       | 40    |                |
| Percentage       | × .80 |                |
| Handicap         | 32.0  | Drop fractions |

## THE SPORT EXPERIENCE

1. Diego has game scores of 159, 146, 165, 176, 156, 141, 183, 143, 158, and 135. What is his average?

2. Lorna has game scores of 143, 158, 135, 159, 146, 165, 141, and 163. What is her average?

3. Janice, Loretta, Conrad, and Steve are entering a league. Their averages are 159, 165, 141, and 183. What is their team average?

Check your answers with those in Appendix D.

easier to use when the bowler's averages change from week to week or the league uses an individual point system for determining winners.

**Individual Method for Team Handicap**

| Name | Scratch | Aver. | Differ. | Percent. | Handicap |
|------|---------|-------|---------|----------|----------|
| Diane | 180 | 135 | 45 | .8 | 36 |
| Jane | 180 | 170 | 10 | .8 | 8 |
| Marie | 180 | 105 | 75 | .8 | 60 |
| Rose | 180 | 125 | 55 | .8 | 44 |
| Nancy | 180 | 140 | 40 | .8 | 32 |
| Team Handicap | | | | | 180 |

**Team Method for Team Handicap**

| Name | Average |
|------|---------|
| Diane | 135 |
| Jane | 170 |
| Connie | 105 |
| Rose | 125 |
| Nancy | 140 |
| Total | 675 |

Handicap = Scratch (800) − Average (675) = 125 × .8 = 100

League and Tournament Play

In the team method, the averages of all bowlers are added together and then a team handicap is calculated, using a predetermined scratch figure and percentage.

Handicaps are usually calculated from the previous season's averages of twenty-one or more games until twelve to eighteen games have been bowled in the current season. Then the current season's average is used.

Handicap charts are available from the various bowling organizations that simplify the calculation of handicaps.

## League Rules

Teams in a league usually consist of three to five bowlers, although a singles league has only one player on a team and a doubles team has two. In order to begin a game, a team must have a legal lineup. Substitutes may be used to complete a legal lineup or a full lineup.

*Legal Lineups*
at least three eligible players for a five-person team
at least two eligible players for a four-person team
at least two eligible players for a three-person team
at least one eligible player for a two-person team

An *absentee score* can be used when a team has enough players for a *legal* lineup, but not enough for a *full* lineup at the beginning of any game in a series. It consists of the average minus 10 pins of the absent bowler on the team roster. When more than one bowler is absent, the absentee score of the player who has bowled the most games is used. The handicap is based on the absentee's actual average.

When there are not enough players on a team's roster for a *full* lineup, the remaining space on the roster is filled with a vacancy score. A vacancy score is 120 unless the league specifies otherwise. In YABA rules, the vacancy score is the lowest average or averages of the bowlers on the opposing team. The handicap is based on the vacancy score allowed.

Tardy players are allowed to begin in the frame the team is on as specified in the rules of each league.

A substitute can be used to replace a bowler after a game has begun in cases of emergency or disability. The original player may return to the lineup for the *next* game. If no substitute is available, a bowler can count one tenth of the absentee score for each remaining frame in the game.

# THE SPORT EXPERIENCE

1. Alana's average is 159. She wants to enter a league that has a scratch figure of 180 and a percentage of 90. What is her handicap for that league?

2. Bob's average is 183. He wants to enter a tournament that has a scratch figure of 200 and a percentage of 80. What is his handicap for the tournament?

3. Doug, Geniece, Larry, and Mossi are competing in a handicap league in which averages are computed by the individual method of team handicapping. Their averages are 159, 165, 183, and 135 respectively. The scratch figure is 200 and the percentage is 70. What is their team handicap?

4. Valais, Loni, Ben, and Charles are entering a league that uses the individual method for determining team handicaps. The scratch figure is 200 and the percentage is 80. What will be their team handicap if their averages are 165, 141, 156, and 176 respectively?

5. Elaine, Linda, Marshall, and Cory have averages of 135, 158, 143, and 183 respectively. What will their handicap be in a league that uses the team method for determining handicaps? The scratch figure for the league is 800 and the percentage is 75.

6. Michelle, Jay, Carol, and Norman are competing in a handicap league in which averages are computed by the team method of handicapping. Their averages are 176, 141, 163, and 146 respectively. The scratch figure is 800 and the percentage is 90. What is their team handicap?

Check your answers with those in Appendix D.

*League and Tournament Play*

Three consecutive games, called a *series*, are bowled by each team every time the league meets. (Youth may bowl one, two, or three games each session.) Teams are arranged in pairs on adjacent lanes. The bowlers of each team begin the first game on the lane to which their team is assigned. After bowling one frame, they switch lanes with the other team and bowl the second frame on the other lane. They continue alternating lanes until the game has been completed. Bonus balls in the tenth frame are taken on the same lane as the first ball of that frame. If there is a vacancy on the team, a *pacer* may fill in to balance the team rotation, but scores made by the pacer do not count in league statistics. In the second and third games of the series, bowlers begin on the lane on which their team finished the preceding game. Teams bowl on different lanes each week until each team has bowled on all lanes.

The order of players in the lineup may be changed at the beginning of any game. Usually, the best bowler rolls last and is called the anchor. The lead-off bowler is usually the second best bowler, with the weakest bowlers in the middle of the lineup.

Whenever a dispute arises and a protest is to be filed, a provisional ball or frame shall be bowled with the same set-up of pins standing at the time of the dispute. Protests must be made in writing within fifteen days of the event or within 48 hours during the last two weeks of the season.

Leagues generally determine team positions on the basis of games won and lost. Popular methods include the four, seven, and individual point systems shown here. Ties count as half a win and half a loss.

## Sample Point System for Determining Team Positions

*Four point system:*
> One point for each game won by a team (1 × 3 games = 3)
> One point for the team with the highest total series score

*Seven point system:*
> Two points for each game won by a team (2 × 3 games = 6)
> One point for the team with the highest total series score

*Individual point system:*
> One point for the individual winners of each game (each player is paired by position with a player on the opposite team, i.e., lead-off bowler with lead-off bowler):

*x* points to the winning team in each game
*x* points to the winning team of the series

The number of points for each game or series is determined by each league. An example might be as follows:

| Team | Ind./Game | Team/Game | Total Game Pts. | Series | Total |
|------|-----------|-----------|-----------------|--------|-------|
| 5 person | 1 × 5 | 4 | 5 × 3 + 4 × 3 | 3 | 30 |
| 4 person | 1 × 4 | 3 | 4 × 3 + 3 × 3 | 1 | 22 |
| 3 person | 1 × 3 | 2 | 3 × 3 + 2 × 3 | 1 | 16 |

An example of the individual point system in a handicap league is provided below.

## BOWLING TOURNAMENTS

A *tournament* is a prearranged event between individuals, teams, or both. Like leagues, tournaments can be scratch, classified, or handicap events. In a handicap or classified tournament, the average submitted must be the bowler's highest average including current season play or an adjusted average as determined by the ABC rules. A beginner with no average may be assigned an average of not less than 165 for women or 170 for men, or the beginner may bowl without a handicap.

| Date _____ 19__ League_____ |||||| Team B |||||| Lane 4 |
|---|---|---|---|---|---|---|---|---|---|---|---|---|
| Team A |||||| 3 ||||||| 
| HDCP | Players | 1st Game | 2nd Game | 3rd Game | Total | HDCP | Players | 1st Game | 2nd Game | 3rd Game | Total |
| 21 | Janet Johnson | (173) | 127 | (179) | 479 | 36 | Elaine White | 140 | (143) | 155 | 438 |
| 17 | Bonnie Bird | 169 | (194) | (142) | 505 | 22 | Karma Evans | (175) | 173 | 117 | 465 |
| 32 | Renee Baker | 118 | 124 | (176) | 418 | 36 | Ann Lastowski | (152) | (144) | 152 | 448 |
| 24 | Dana Palmer | 150 | 150 | 109 | 409 | 45 | Karen Coombs | (130) | (179) | (168) | 477 |
| 25 | Ruth King | (137) | (145) | (170) | 452 | 37 | Kathy Stokes | 124 | 132 | 127 | 383 |
| | Total Subtotal | 747 | 740 | 776 | 2263 | | Total Subtotal | 721 | 771 | 719 | 2211 |
| | HDCP Handicap | 119 | 119 | 119 | 357 | | HDCP Handicap | 176 | 176 | 176 | 528 |
| Won 10 | Total INC HDCP | 866 | 859 | 895 | 2620 | Won 20 | Total INC HDCP | 897 | 947 | 895 | (2739) |
| Lost 20 | Game won by indicate by X in square | | | Tie | | Lost 10 | Game won by indicate by X in square | X | X | Tie | |

Signed __Karen Coombs__  
Opposing Team Captain

Signed __Janet Johnson__  
Opposing Team Captain

**Sample individual point system**

*League and Tournament Play*

# THE SPORT EXPERIENCE

Join a bowling league and make a record of your own scores and your team's win-loss record.

---

No absentee or vacancy scores may be used in tournament play. Missed frames are scored as zeros. Tardy players may begin play and score points in the frame currently being bowled. In case of emergency or disability after the game begins, a substitute may be used as described in league play.

Tournaments often consist of a team event, a doubles event, and a singles event. A player who participates in all of these events is eligible for an all-events prize.

## Fun Tournaments

The following fun tournaments can be played with teams of from two to four players:

***Bridge Tournament.*** Each player scores only the number of pins knocked down—no strikes or spares. After each frame, winners move up and losers move down. The winner on the top lane remains on the top lane; the loser on the bottom lane remains on the bottom lane. Middle players on a team, if any, remain where they are.

| 1 | 2 | 3 | 4 | 5 | 6 |
|---|---|---|---|---|---|
| W stays<br>L → | ←W<br>L → | ←W<br>L → | ←W<br>L → | ←W<br>L → | ←W<br>L stays |

***Strikes and Spares.*** Each player has two rolls in each frame. A strike on the first ball allows the player to try for another strike on the second ball. Score 10 points for each strike and 5 points for each spare. The team with the highest score wins (Kidwell, Kathro, and Paul Smith, Jr., *Bowling Analyzed*. Dubuque, Iowa: Wm. C. Brown Company Publishers, 1960, p. 82).

***Play-Off.*** Each player on the team bowls one frame of a game in order. Repeat until an entire game has been played (i.e., frame 1—player A, frame 2—player B, 3—C, 4—D, 5—E, 6—player A again, 7—B, etc.). The team with the highest score wins.

***Headpin Tournament.*** Each player has 12 turns of one ball per frame. Score 10 points if the headpin is knocked down by the ball; 0 if not hit. The player or team with the highest score is the winner (Shunk, Carol, *Bowling*, third edition. San Francisco: Saunders College Publishing, 1983, p. 82).

***Dutch Couples.*** One player rolls the first ball of the frame and the other player rolls the second ball. Alternate every frame. The couple with the highest score is the winner (Shunk, p. 82).

***Family Tournament.*** All members of the family bowl together. The total or combined score of all members is kept. Each time the family bowls, they try to improve the total family score.

## Marking

The more marks you bowl in a game, the higher your score will be. Note the number of marks required to bowl the following scores (American Association for Health, Physical Education, and Recreation, *New Ideas for Bowling Instruction*, 1970, p. 48):

| Marks | Score | Marks | Score |
| --- | --- | --- | --- |
| 1 | 91–103 | 6 | 144–153 |
| 2 | 104–113 | 7 | 154–163 |
| 3 | 114–123 | 8 | 164–173 |
| 4 | 124–133 | 9 | 174–183 |
| 5 | 134–143 | 10 | 184 and up |

Some bowlers like to know how their team is doing against another team in league or tournament play. However, because strikes and spares cannot be scored until bonus balls are rolled, it is not easy to total each frame to compare scores. To accomplish this a system of counting marks has been developed. Each strike or spare counts one mark. A strike preceded by a strike earns a bonus mark so it is worth two marks. Marks are lost when a bowler fails to pick up at least five pins on the bonus balls needed to score the marks.

Let's look at a game and see how marking works. Before starting the game, the handicaps are divided by 10 to get the starting marks. (round your answer to the nearest whole number). Adam and Betty are playing in a mixed doubles league against Carl and Diane. Divide

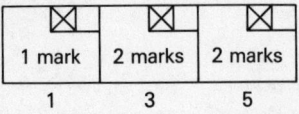

| ⊠ | ⊠ | ⊠ |
|---|---|---|
| 1 mark | 2 marks | 2 marks |
| 1 | 3 | 5 |

One mark for each single strike or spare
Two marks for each consecutive strike (1 + 1 bonus)

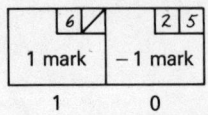

| 6 / | 2 | 5 |
|---|---|---|
| 1 mark | −1 mark |
| 1 | 0 |

Lose one mark by failing to knock down at least five pins:
On the first ball following a spare

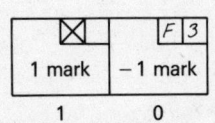

| ⊠ | F | 3 |
|---|---|---|
| 1 mark | −1 mark |
| 1 | 0 |

On both balls following a strike

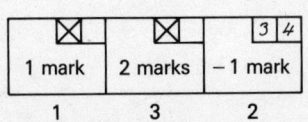

| ⊠ | ⊠ | 3 | 4 |
|---|---|---|---|
| 1 mark | 2 marks | −1 mark |
| 1 | 3 | 2 |

On first ball following a multiple strike

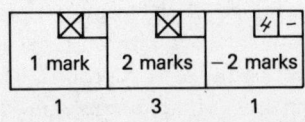

| ⊠ | ⊠ | 4 | − |
|---|---|---|---|
| 1 mark | 2 marks | −2 marks |
| 1 | 3 | 1 |

Lose two marks by failing to knock down at least five pins on both balls following a multiple strike.

**Figuring marks**

| Name | | 1 | 2 | 3 | 4 | 5 | 6 | 7 | 8 | 9 | 10 | Total |
|---|---|---|---|---|---|---|---|---|---|---|---|---|
| | | | | | | | | | | | | Hcp 111 |
| Adam | 59 | 3 / | 1 / | 4 4 | 8 / | X | 5 / | 6 / | 2 / | 5 / | 7 / 4 | |
| | | 11 | 25 | 33 | 53 | 69 | 75 | 87 | 102 | 119 | 133 | 244 |
| Betty | 52 | X | 4 / | X | X | G 3 | 3 / | 2 / | X | 2 3 | X 6 | |
| | | 20 | 40 | 60 | 63 | 66 | 70 | 90 | 105 | 110 | 130 | 374 |
| Marks per frame | | +½ | +½ | +1 | | +3 | +1 | | +½ | +½ | +1 | |
| Marks | 11 | 13 | 14 | 14 | 17 | 16 | 16 | 18 | 19 | 20 | | |

| Name | | 1 | 2 | 3 | 4 | 5 | 6 | 7 | 8 | 9 | 10 | Total |
|---|---|---|---|---|---|---|---|---|---|---|---|---|
| | | | | | | | | | | | | Hcp 84 |
| Carl | 21 | 3 3 | X | 4 / | X | X | 8 / | 5 / | X | 2 / | X 2 7 | |
| | | 6 | 26 | 46 | 74 | 94 | 109 | 129 | 149 | 169 | 188 | 272 |
| Diane | 63 | 5 / | 3 / | 1 / | X | 4 – | G / | 1 7 | 4 / | 9 / | 4 / X | |
| | | 13 | 24 | 44 | 58 | 62 | 73 | 81 | 100 | 114 | 134 | 406 |
| Marks per frame | | +1 | +½ | +½ | +2 | +½ | +2 | +1 | +2 | +2 | | |
| Marks | 8 | 9 | 10 | 11 | 13 | 14 | 16 | 16 | 18 | 20 | | |

**Example of marking**

Adam's and Betty's handicaps by 10 to get their starting marks (111 ÷ 10 = 11.1, rounded off to 11). Carl and Diane begin with 8 marks (21 + 63 = 84 ÷ 10 = 8).

Adam and Betty earn two marks in the first frame (a spare and a strike). With the eleven marks from the handicaps, their running score is thirteen marks. Carl and Diane have one spare, which makes their running score 9.

In the second frame, Adam loses the mark he gained in frame 1 by failing to knock down at least five pins on the first ball following a spare. However, he and Betty earn two marks for their spares, so they add one mark (2 − 1 = 1) to their running score, yielding 14. Diane also loses one mark for knocking down only three pins on her first ball after a spare. With their two earned marks, they also add one mark to their running score.

Each team loses a mark in frame 3 for knocking down less than five pins on the first ball after a spare. Adam and Betty gain one mark so their running score remains the same. Carl and Diane gain two marks so they add 1 to their running score.

In frame 4, Betty earns a bonus mark for a strike preceded by a strike. Her two marks (1 + 1 bonus), plus Adam's spare, bring the running score to 17. Diane and Carl add two marks for their strikes.

Adam adds one mark in frame 5. Betty loses a mark for her gutter ball on the first ball following a multiple strike and another one for

*League and Tournament Play*

# THE SPORT EXPERIENCE

Than and Maria are playing Denise and Ron in a doubles tournament. Score the game and figure the marks for both teams. Check your answers with those in Appendix D.

| Name | 1 | 2 | 3 | 4 | 5 | 6 | 7 | 8 | 9 | 10 | Total |
|---|---|---|---|---|---|---|---|---|---|---|---|
| Than | 6 / | 2 / | X | 5 / | 8 1 | X | X | 4 / | X | F 3 | 27 |
| Maria | F / | 2 / | X | X | 5 / | 6 9 | 8 / | X | 2 1 | 3 / 4 | 36 |
| marks | | | | | | | | | | | |

| Name | 1 | 2 | 3 | 4 | 5 | 6 | 7 | 8 | 9 | 10 | Total |
|---|---|---|---|---|---|---|---|---|---|---|---|
| Denise | X | 2 2 | 6 / | X | 6 / | 5 / | F 9 | X | X | 4 / X | 18 |
| Ron | X | 3 1 | X | X | 6 / | X | 9 / | 2 / | F 8 | 3 4 | 31 |
| marks | | | | | | | | | | | |

failing to knock down five pins on both balls following a strike. Thus, you will note that failure to get at least five pins on both balls following a multiple strike always results in losing two marks. Carl gets two marks for his strike preceded by a strike, but Diane loses one for failing to get five pins on two balls following her strike.

In frame 6, Adam and Betty do not gain or lose any marks. Carl and Diane pick up two marks with their spares. Follow the rest of the marks and see if you can determine why each was won or lost. Notice that they stopped counting marks in the ninth frame. In the tenth frame, each team's scores become evident. The players' scores in the totals column are added together, along with the handicap, to create a running score as the players finish their games.

# 5

# Strategies for the Advanced Bowler

Now that you have some experience bowling, you have undoubtedly discovered that variations in bowling lanes and equipment can make a big difference at the higher levels of competition. This chapter presents some of the strategies for dealing with these conditions.

## READING THE LANES

When your ball rolls over the usual target and still misses the pocket, lane conditions have changed. Conditions can change due to dust, dressing, humidity, temperature, and time of day. Lanes also differ due to wood texture, finish, or slickness.

Reading the lanes requires some knowledge of the sections of the lanes. The sections are: (1) the approach, (2) the heads, (3) the 45-foot section from the arrows to the pin deck, and (4) the pin deck.

The approach is the area where the bowler's delivery takes place. What is the condition of the approach? Is it slippery? Is it sticky? These factors affect the bowler's balance. The first thing to do if the approach surface doesn't please you is to check the surface of your shoes. Make sure the soles of your shoes are clean and dry. If this does not solve the problem, ask the desk attendant at the bowling center to correct the problem on the approach surface.

The heads are the first fifteen feet of the lane beyond the foul line. This is where the ball starts its path to the pins. The bowler has no control over the ball after it lands on the heads. The ball surface starts to react with the lane surface and the lane conditioning or dressing. This reaction can vary immensely from one lane to another. The grain of the boards and the dressing or oil on the lanes may affect the desired reaction between the ball and the lane. The desired reaction of the ball is to skid, roll, and hook before it hits the pins. Lane reading involves determining the skid, roll, and hook of your ball. This is determined to a large extent by the way the lanes are oiled. Oiling has two purposes—to protect the lanes, and to create shots. The heads are covered with lacquer or some other substance to protect against the pounding of the ball at contact. They are sometimes double-oiled. Heavy oiling will decrease the amount of hook.

The area from the arrows to the pin deck is where you need to determine what the conditioning has to do with the travel of the ball. If the oil has been applied only fifteen or twenty feet down the lane, the ball will roll and hook early. This makes it difficult to hit the pocket if you hook the ball. If the lane is oiled down thirty to thirty-five feet, your ball will have a good skid, roll, and hook pattern. If it is oiled more than thirty-five feet, it becomes difficult to hook the ball and makes it harder to get the desired angle to the pins.

You need to determine what is happening so you can make adjustments. Should you increase or decrease speed? Should you change your angle? Does the ball need to hook sooner or later, or more or less? These adjustments will be discussed in the next section.

The other thing to determine is how much oil lies around the lane. Are there dry areas? Is one area more heavily oiled than another? To determine where the oil is on the lanes, you need to roll the ball a few times. You need to change targets and lines to the pocket. Each time watch the skid, roll, and hook of the ball. If the pattern is different on different sections of the lane, you will know the oil is different if everything else remains the same. Rolling the ball in a dry area will increase the hook; while in an area with more oil, the hook will be less.

An even lane has the lane oiled from gutter to gutter. On a blocked lane, however, the center boards from the second arrow from the right to the second arrow from the left are oiled heavily thirty-five to forty feet beyond the foul line. The boards outside the second arrows are lightly oiled down twenty-five to thirty feet. The light oil provides enough oil for skid and the heavy oil stops the hook and guides the ball into the pocket. In this circumstance you would want your target to be closer to the gutter than the second arrow.

Another factor to determine when reading the lane is lane track. This is the area of the most play on the lane. It is usually somewhere between the first and third arrows, sometimes as narrow as the eighth to twelfth boards. It varies from lane to lane and house to house. The ball will grip the lane and hook more strongly when it is in the track. If

# THE SPORT EXPERIENCE

Watch the angle at which the ball contacts the pocket. Determine the angle of deflection of the ball. Does it continue to drive through the pocket and blow the 5 pin away? Where does the ball leave the pin deck? To answer these questions requires that you watch the ball carefully.

---

you can play the track and your ball is hooking too much, move your target inside the track so your ball will enter the track farther down the lane. If the ball isn't hooking enough, move the target closer to the gutter and play into the track sooner. The majority of bowlers are right-handed, so the conditions change more rapidly for them. Because only about 5 percent of bowlers are left-handed, there is no ball track on the left side of bowling lanes.

The pin deck is where the reaction between the ball and the pins occurs. If the ball misses the pocket, you will need to adjust. If the ball deflects too much you may need to use a heavier ball or improve your release. The correct release will add explosive power as the ball drives into the pins. You may need to change balls. If you desire to develop this skill, watch carefully and don't be afraid to change when you need to.

If you aren't striking and you are losing, what have you got to lose if you change? Watch what happens as the ball rolls down the lane and collect the information available at the pin deck and make your adjustments. Keep practicing and the ability to read the lanes will be added to your bowling skills.

## ADJUSTING TO LANE CONDITIONS

There are two ways to adjust to the lanes. The first way is to move your target or your feet. The second way is to change your delivery. The easiest way is to move your feet and keep the same spot, although changing your spot is also easy. Both involve a left or right movement on the lane or approach. Changes in delivery require you to change ball speed, change your release, apply more or less lift, or change the amount of loft on the ball. These are very complicated adjustments

*Strategies for the Advanced Bowler*

Slow lane

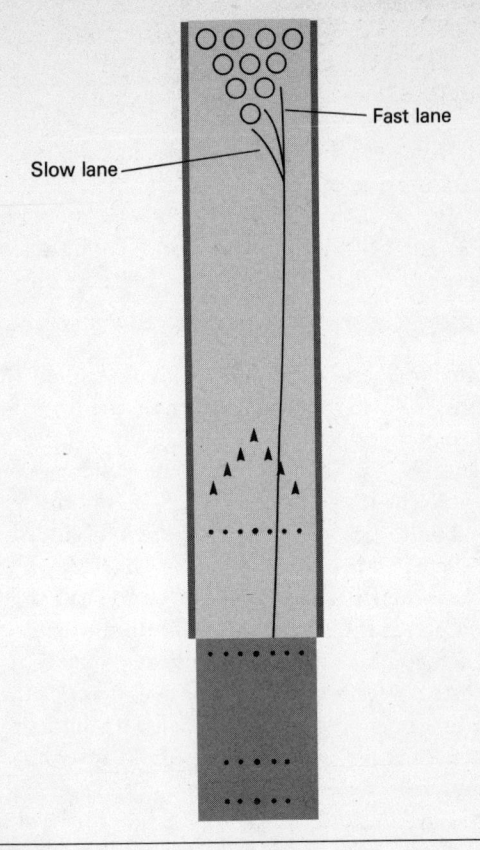

Fast lane

**Lane conditions**

and usually require a high level of skill to make the changes and maintain a consistent percentage of pocket hits. Unless you practice a great deal, make your adjustments by moving.

Many bowlers have only one ball or use a house ball. They also do not practice enough to control changes in delivery. If this is true for you, stick with the movement of your feet and the movement of your spot. Learn to control the movement adjustments while you develop good solid fundamentals. Don't stay in the same spot and fight the conditions. Learn to read the lane and adjust to the conditions on the lane. When you understand how to make the simple adjustments and have a high average, then develop your delivery changes.

Try some of the activities listed below for adjusting to the lanes to determine their effects.

1. If the ball hooks too late or too little:
   a. Move your feet toward the outside of the lane and move your target closer to the gutter.
   b. Reduce loft. Place the ball down close to the foul line.
   c. Reduce ball speed by slowing the approach speed. This is done by shortening your steps and your armswing. You may also slow down your follow-through.
   d. Use a softer ball (see the next section).
   e. Use more lift by emphasizing the squeeze on the release and accelerating the follow-through.

2. If the ball hooks too early:
   a. Move your feet toward the center of the lane and move your target closer to the fourth arrow.
   b. Loft the ball out on the lane.
   c. Increase ball speed by lengthening your steps and armswing and accelerating the follow-through.
   d. Use a harder ball (see the next section).
   e. Use less lift by decreasing the amount of squeeze and the speed of the follow-through.

Reading the lanes and adjusting to them go hand-in-hand. Make a good marriage of the two and keep them together. Each time you practice, try to determine where the oil lies on the lanes so you can make the best adjustments.

## EQUIPMENT CHANGES

The subject of equipment changes can be a very complex one, but it is better for nonprofessional bowlers to keep it simple. Learn to read the lanes or it will be impossible to make the right choices about your equipment. The purpose of equipment changes is to more effectively

## THE SPORT EXPERIENCE

If you have more than one ball, experiment on varying lane conditions. Watch the skid, roll, and hook patterns of each ball. Try different targets and determine which ball works best for the various lane conditions and lines to the pocket. You may have to bowl at different bowling centers. You might find different conditions later in the evening than in the morning, so vary your practice times.

---

hit the pocket or convert spares. Bowling balls differ in composition, surface hardness and softness, and in the way they are weighted. These differences will cause different reactions with the lane surface.

The hardness of the ball will affect the skid, roll, and hook pattern of the ball. Soft balls will hook more than hard balls. Soft plastic will usually skid more and hook later and less than a rubber ball of similar hardness. Hard plastic balls will usually skid less and hook earlier and more than a rubber ball of the same degree of hardness.

Various ball weights also affect the ball's reaction to the lanes. A ball can be as light as eight pounds or as heavy as sixteen pounds. Choose a weight you can handle. Males often choose the maximum weight when they would be wiser to use a fourteen or fifteen pound ball. Forget your ego and improve your scores. No one cares how much your ball weighs. Get strikes if you want to impress other bowlers.

There are many combinations of ball weighting. They are determined by how the ball is drilled in relation to the weight block of the ball. Drilling the fingers closer to the trademark will result in finger weight; closer to the thumb results in thumb weight. Drilling the holes to the right or left side results in negative or positive side weights. There are also top and bottom weights which are related to the weight block built into the ball. The weight block weighs more than the normal ball material; therefore, by positioning the holes differently, the reaction between the balls and the lanes will differ.

Top, finger, and right-side weights are positive weights. Positive weights usually delay the hook, generate more hook, and create a greater driving force through the pins.

Bottom, thumb, and left-side weights are negative weights. With negative weight the ball hooks sooner, the hook is less, and the deflection is greater upon contact with the pins. Ball weight has a tremendous effect upon patterns of ball roll and is a complex subject. Don't be concerned with it unless you have high aspirations as a bowler.

To use the strategies learned in this chapter in your bowling game you must make some choices. First, change your shoes. Choose the ball you are going to use. Determine your target method of aiming. Decide on the spot or spots you will use. Position yourself on the approach. Remember where you started so you can duplicate it on the next shot. You will already know the ball roll pattern you use. Use it for all of the balls you roll. Make your approach and delivery. Make your release properly. Roll the ball over your spot or spots. Hit the pocket and get a strike. If this happens, duplicate it over and over. If it doesn't, convert your spare. Now make your adjustments.

The most common adjustment is to move your feet so you will get the ball solidly in the pocket. Even when you hit the pocket you may determine you didn't like the skid, roll, and hook pattern of the ball. You can decide to move your feet and your target so you have a slightly or vastly different line to the pocket. The different line may give you the skid, roll, and hook you desire. If the change doesn't help, you may want to make an equipment change if you own more than one ball. Make an intelligent choice based on your knowledge of your balls. If these changes don't get you lined up or if you are hitting the pocket, but are not getting strikes, you can make a delivery change if you have acquired the skill. If you don't have the skill, don't add to your confusion by making unintelligent changes.

# Playing the Mental Game

Bowlers often have one of two common misconceptions. One is, "I know what I am doing so I don't need to practice." The other is, "Bowling is a physical game so all I need to do to get better is practice." Both approaches have serious flaws. Bowling is a game made of simple physical skills and complex mental skills. Bowlers who think they don't need to practice and don't practice will find that fatigue will take away from their scores in a long competition. The tension or pressures of competition demand that bowlers be in good mental and physical condition. Bowlers who do practice, but fail to develop a proper set of mental skills will be destroyed when they compete with the masters of the game. Don't let either of these misconceptions stop you from the success you desire. Develop both physical and mental skills for your bowling game.

Playing the mental game is a combination of knowledge and attitude. Knowledge is the determining factor in developing ability and skills, but attitude can determine whether or not you effectively utilize your abilities and skills.

Knowledge includes the information required to make wise decisions about your game. Most people believe that anyone can bowl. It is true that most people can roll the ball down the lane. It is an entirely different matter to roll the ball consistently, accurately, and with effective power. It is no simple matter to select the best equipment, develop a line to the pocket, and learn the most effective delivery technique. Making a less than wise decision on any of these factors could cause you to bowl a lower score than your opponent.

People often hear in bowling centers, "That bowler has a great physical game, but a weak mental game," or "I was bowling great, but I just couldn't get going mentally." Would you rather admit you are weak mentally or weak physically? If either is weak, both are weak because one has such a dramatic effect on the other. Nothing could be better for a bowler's mental game than to be lined up, relaxed, and making high scores.

Tom Baker and Pete Weber, two touring professionals, both bowled 300 games in match play in Denver, Colorado. You only need to watch one match like that to realize one small error physically or mentally will cause defeat. As you develop your bowling game, you must prepare mentally as well as physically to be a great competitor in bowling. Practice your mental skills just as you do your physical skills.

## CONFIDENCE

One of the most important attributes to develop is confidence in your ability to bowl well. Confidence comes from knowledge, skill, and attitude. Confidence requires knowledge about your possible choices. This can happen through experience. An easy way is to converse with someone who already has the knowledge. First learn, then apply that knowledge. Spend some time gaining your own understanding, then go back to your advisor and talk again. Experience and a good teacher can expand your knowledge rapidly. With the rapid expansion of knowledge, you will develop a sense of confidence. Now you are prepared to make wise choices with confidence.

To develop confidence in your bowling skills, attempt to identify the feeling you have when you have a successful approach and delivery and then duplicate that feeling each time you bowl. Develop a relaxed delivery, with just the right amount of acceleration at the release.

Develop sound skills and then trust yourself to use them. Set realistic goals for yourself. Determine what you want to happen and allow your body to do it. Don't force yourself because if you do you will be disappointed in the way you respond. When you compete, don't try to be perfect. You aren't perfect in practice so don't worry about it in competition. Your competitors are not perfect either. Professional bowlers consider a 200 game a par game. They are the best in the world, and yet they consider two-thirds of the possible points as par. It is very rare that a professional averages over 218 for a complete

# THE SPORT EXPERIENCE

Practice the following activities to develop confidence in your bowling skills:

1. Walk through your approach and delivery and feel it. Now try to repeat as closely as possible the exact feeling. Don't be concerned with what happens, just feel it. Can you allow it to feel the same? The word *allow* was chosen because you must not try to make it happen. You must allow it to happen. Each time, determine how the attempt felt and duplicate the feeling. Identify how it feels in different parts of the armswing and duplicate the feeling. Make the same determination about the footwork and repeat the feeling. Don't attempt to make physical changes. Attempt to change the feeling until it can be repeated over and over. This is much harder than just rolling the ball down the lane. Become aware of the ball at all points of the delivery. Feel the ball at all times while it is in contact with your hand or hands.

2. Practice the armswing to feel the relaxation. Without the ball, raise your right arm in front of your body to shoulder level. Hold the right arm with your left hand. Relax the right arm as much as you can. Remove the left hand. If you remained in a state of relaxation, your right arm dropped effortlessly down past your body and up into your backswing. Now, hold the right arm in the backswing and relax it and it will move forward and down in an effortless swing.

3. Sit down and try to picture in your mind and feel in your body the relaxation in the swing that you just experienced. Do the exercise again with your ball or a lighter object. Visualize your experience, concentrating on relaxation. You can approach it another way. Use your ball, but start the swing from a lower position and increase the height as you become comfortable.

4. Now, go through your approach and delivery and release the ball while concentrating on a relaxed armswing. The

forearm and fingers may remain tense, but relax the muscles that affect the shoulder joint movement. The weight of the ball is enough to allow movement to occur at the shoulder joint.

5. Practice the acceleration at the point of release. Start with the right heel positioned in the third step and the ball at the top of the backswing. Simultaneously move the ball and plant the right toe. The ball continues and the fourth step occurs. With all the effort you have, accelerate the arm, hand, and ball through your release. Visualize and attempt to feel the experience. Do the same thing with the full armswing. To do a proper armswing, you must relax. During the armswing, concentrate on relaxation until the point of release, then concentrate on acceleration. Acceleration is important at the release in order to apply the force of the total approach and delivery into the ball. This is necessary for explosive power at the pins. The more you relax, the greater you can accelerate. Practice until you can get the relaxation to blend into the acceleration.

---

season. Develop the ability to let your body do what you have trained it to do. Don't let a past error affect your next ball.

Excellent performance occurs when the bowler seems to be somewhere else, but is still totally involved with his or her game. Some say that this is complete or total concentration. Learn this state of mind and you will have mastery of one more of the mental aspects of bowling. Concentration is the ability to become so involved with something that nothing else is noticed. Become aware of every aspect of your physical game. Become so aware that you know immediately if something is wrong. Concentrate your attention and focus all your energy into the release. It is extremely important that you learn to concentrate on the release. Learn to make everything come together at the release. Become aware of any errors so they can be corrected before the release or compensated for by the release. Do you increase or decrease lift? Do you pull the ball inside your mark a board or two or do you swing it out a board or two? When you develop your concentration, you will learn to compensate automatically.

Confidence also comes from identifying with your successes. Unsuccessful attempts must be viewed as an opportunity to learn what not to do. After learning, eliminate them from your mind. Both success and failure are learning experiences and how they are handled is what makes the bowler. As you eliminate judgments of good and bad, you begin to trust yourself to gain your desires.

## COMPENSATION

The phenomenon of compensation may be the single most important skill to develop in bowling. It is the amazing ability of the mind and body, when working together, to compensate for errors and bring about the desired effect. It, too, is a blend of knowledge, skills, and attitudes. It brings pinpoint accuracy when shooting at an area. It brings the confidence needed to make choices about equipment and adjustments to lane conditions. It is sensing and feeling. It is knowing. Those who have it become winners. Those who don't have it struggle to become winners, but never have the opportunity. Program yourself by practicing the activities presented in this book for developing physical and mental skills; then allow the phenomenon of compensation to operate while you compete.

The bowler who has taken the time to develop mental skills beyond the development of a solid physical game has the competitive edge. A good knowledge of fundamental physical principles is definitely part of the mental game, but the ability to trust your knowledge and skills must exist before the ability to compensate can exist consistently. Top bowlers have such a perfect blend of the mind and body that it is difficult to understand where the power comes from. It is a quality often referred to as greatness.

Pinpoint accuracy occurs because of confidence in what you know, a relaxed delivery, and the ability to trust your skills. Confidence follows the knowledge that errors can and will be corrected by the amazing ability of the mind and body to compensate. As you come to a knowledge that no one bowls without errors, both physical and mental, but that the errors can be corrected before you release the ball, you will be more relaxed. Your relaxation will allow you to roll or stroke the ball rather than throw it. Your physical skills will improve, especially your timing. Your scores will be higher. Your confidence will be greater. You will then trust yourself. You will allow yourself to be more aggressive. Your ball will be released more effectively. You will have a straight approach and armswing. Your ball roll pattern will improve. You will be able to make strikes with different pocket hits. You will carry the light hits, the pocket hits, and the high hits. This will happen because of the increased pin action.

With the ability to hit your mark easily, you will have the ability to make wise choices about changing equipment or making adjustments on the lane to more effectively use the lane conditions.

The mental game becomes powerful when you truly understand the amazing ability to compensate. When you gain this understanding and have a solid physical game, you are equipped to become truly phenomenal.

# 7
# Where Do You Go from Here?

Bowling is an activity which you can participate in and enjoy for your entire life regardless of your bowling skills. You will meet many people who can be your friends if you choose to allow them the opportunity. If you enjoy competition, there is always someone else who enjoys competing in bowling. The handicap system will make it possible to compete with people of different abilities. If you enjoy a challenge, you can find many challenges in bowling. Bowling is a demanding game, which no one has yet conquered. You can learn to strike, but not every time. Friendships, competition, challenge, and your own desires and goals in bowling will keep you going for at least a lifetime, even if it is a long, happy one.

Where you go from here depends on where you are and where you desire to go. Your success depends on your desire and your motivation to pay the price for success. The price will include money spent for bowling, instruction, and equipment. Time devoted to practice, participation in leagues and tournaments, and traveling time to and from the bowling center is also part of the price. Mental and physical stress, resulting from success and failure, will be included in the price you pay.

You have the information required to get an excellent start on your goals. You may just want to socialize. If so, you need to pay the cost of bowling equipment, transportation, and time for your socializing. There are millions of people who bowl in many leagues and tournaments across America and throughout the world. They come from many walks of life. Bowl and have fun with your friends at the bowling center.

You may restrict your bowling to a little practice time and the social life around leagues and tournaments, but you may want to be competitive in your bowling. Then the price is higher. You will probably need to spend some time in serious practice. You could make yourself competitive sooner by spending some time with a qualified bowling teacher. Be prepared to pay for the instructor's time and talent. This could be in private lessons or in group lessons. The instructor may not give you any more information than this book offers, but he or she can give you the personal touch. Some bowling centers and many colleges of physical education offer instruction in bowling. You will also have to pay the price of some stress.

You may have even higher aspirations of becoming the best bowler in your local bowling center, your state, or in the country. You are now considering becoming a highly competitive bowler. To become the best in your local center is very hard if any high caliber bowlers also compete at your local center. If you desire this, be prepared to pay the price. It is high, but it can also be exciting, rewarding, and satisfying. You will love it. You will hate it. You will have moments of great confidence. You will experience moments of frustration. Continue your pursuit and you will learn, you will grow, and you will realize your goals. You will succeed.

Develop a regular schedule for practice. Be consistent. No one can tell you exactly what to do to succeed at bowling. You can gather excellent ideas and put them in your program and determine the results. Some suggestions that may help you reach these higher goals follow:

1. Determine your exact goals.

2. Reevaluate and modify your goals regularly.

3. Practice! Practice! Practice!

4. Learn when to stop practicing and get away. Practicing when you are fatigued may be more detrimental than constructive.

5. Program yourself for the competitive situation.

6. Build your confidence.

7. Control your emotions.

8. Be willing to change. You must change to get better.

9. Learn to overcome your fears.

10. Trust your body to do what you have practiced.

11. Learn how the other aspects of your life contribute to your success or failure in bowling (i.e., diet, exercise, emotional reactions, human relationships).

12. Become fit physically, mentally, emotionally, and spiritually.

**SPORT FOR LIFE** has a selection of excellent texts on a variety of sports. Learning to bowl should encourage you to embark on a life filled with physical activity. Once you have accepted the challenge to develop skills in one sport, you will find it easier to learn other sports. The physical skills may be very different, but the mental skills you have learned will apply almost directly to anything else in life you choose. If you choose some other sports, you will find that the variety will keep you fresh and your enthusiasm high.

It is important to have an activity that you enjoy to use as a form of relaxation. If you choose to take bowling seriously, you might want to choose a sport with defensive tactics, such as tennis, basketball, karate, or fencing. Bowling is a sport utilizing only offense. Sports with defensive tactics may help you in competition. You will also improve your physical conditioning if you choose to relax away from bowling by engaging in another sport. Running or weight training will also add to your overall body conditioning. If you are going to be competitive in bowling, choose at least one other sport that is strictly for enjoyment and relaxation.

# Appendix A
# *Bowling Dictionary*

**ABC** American Bowling Congress, governing body for men's bowling
**Alley** a lane
**Anchor** last bowler on a team, usually the best bowler
**Approach** part of the lane behind the foul line from which the bowler's approach is made
**Arrows** spots on the lane at which the bowler aims
**Average** the sum of the scores of all games bowled in a league or tournament divided by the number of games bowled, rounded to the next lower whole number; usually a minimum of three games for leagues and twenty-one games for tournaments

**Baby split** a 2-7 or 3-10 split
**Backup ball** a ball that curves to the right for a right-handed bowler and to the left for a left-handed bowler
**Ball return** an underground track on which the ball rolls from the pit to the approach
**Bed posts** a 7-10 split
**Big four** a 4-6-7-10 split
**Blind score** score used for an absent player
**Blow** failure to get a strike or spare in a frame unless there is a split
**Body English** movements of the body following the release and follow-through of the delivery
**Brooklyn** a hit to the left of the center of the headpin or in the 1-2 pocket for a right-handed bowler; a hit to the right of the center of the headpin or in the 1-3 pocket for a left-hander
**Bucket** a 2-4-5-8 or 3-5-6-9 leave

**Channel** current team for gutter; a trough for collecting errant balls
**Cherry** knocking down the front pin or pins with the second ball and leaving the rear pin
**Classified league** a league with different divisions, with entrance in each based on the bowlers' averages
**Clothesline** a 1-2-4-7 or 1-3-6-10 pin leave
**Count** the number of pins knocked down by the first ball of a frame; used to score a spare in the previous frame
**Creeper** a very slow ball
**Crossover** Brooklyn

**Curve ball**   a ball that travels in a wide arc toward the pins

**Dead ball**   an ineffective ball that doesn't "work"
**Dead wood**   pins left lying on the lane or in the channel after a delivery
**Diamond**   a bucket
**Double**   two consecutive strikes
**Double balling**   rolling a second ball before the first has been returned; may break the pinsetter
**Double pinochle**   a 4-6-7-10 split
**Dutch 200**   a 200 score made by alternating strikes and spares for the entire ten frames

| 1 | 2 | 3 | 4 | 5 | 6 | 7 | 8 | 9 | 10 | Total |
|---|---|---|---|---|---|---|---|---|---|---|
| ⊠ | ⟋ | ⊠ | ⟋ | ⊠ | ⟋ | ⊠ | ⟋ | ⊠ | ⟋⊠ | |
| 20 | 40 | 60 | 80 | 100 | 120 | 140 | 160 | 180 | 200 | 200 |

**Error**   failure to get a strike or spare in a frame unless there is a split

**Fast lane**   a slick lane that cuts down on the amount of ball hook
**FIQ**   Federation Internationale des Quilleurs—international bowling organization
**Foul**   any part of the body touching anything beyond the foul line, including the floor, wall, or channel
**Foul line**   line separating the approach from the lane
**Frame**   one-tenth of a game; a box on the scoresheet
**Full hit**   ball strikes a pin at or near its center

**Game**   a line; ten frames
**Goal posts**   a 7-10 split
**Graveyards**   lanes that are hard to score on
**Groove**   a very shallow depression on a lane; an expression for a high-scoring lane
**Gutter**   a channel
**Gutter ball**   a ball rolled in the channel or gutter

**Handicap**   an adjustment in scores of individuals or teams to equalize competition
**Headpin**   the 1 pin
**High hit**   a ball that hits on the headpin side of the 1-3 pocket or hits the headpin straight on
**Holding lane**   a fast lane
**Hook**   a ball that breaks sharply to the center of the lane during the last few feet of its approach to the pins
**House ball**   a ball provided by the bowling center

**Inning**　one-tenth of a game; one frame on the scoresheet

**Kegler**　a bowler
**Kickbacks**　sideboards at the pit end of the lane
**Kingpin**　the 5 pin

**Lane**　formerly called alley; the wood surface on which bowling occurs
**Lead-off**　first bowler on a team
**League**　an organized group of teams competing on a regular basis
**Leave**　pins left standing after the first ball of a frame
**Lift**　giving an upward motion to the ball with the fingers during the release
**Light hit**　a ball hitting the side of a target pin causing considerable pin deflection
**Line**　a game
**Line bowling**　visualizing an imaginary line to the pins during delivery
**Loft**　releasing the ball too late causing it to land on the lane some distance from the foul line; this can damage the lane surface
**LPBT**　Ladies Professional Bowlers Tour

**Mark**　a strike or spare
**Miss**　failure to get a strike or spare in a frame unless there is a split
**Mixer**　a ball that produces lots of pin action

**NBC**　National Bowling Council, organization for the bowling industry
**Nose hit**　a ball that hits the headpin straight on, usually resulting in a split such as the 4-10 or 4-6-7-10

**Open frame**　a frame without a mark

**PBA**　Professional Bowlers Association, men's organization
**Perfect game**　300 points, twelve consecutive marks
**Pin bowling**　aiming at the pins when delivering the ball
**Pin deck**　part of the lane on which the pins stand
**Pinsetter**　machine that respots the pins and returns the ball
**Pit**　the depression behind the pin deck into which the pins fall
**Pitch**　the angle at which the thumb and finger holes are drilled in a ball
**Pocket**　space between the 1-3 pins for a right-handed bowler or between the 1-2 pins for a left-handed bowler

**Railroad**　a split
**Rake**　the device that clears the pins off the pin deck after each delivery
**Running lane**　a slow lane on which the ball hooks too much

**Scratch**　using actual scores without handicaps in individual or league competition

**Series**   three or more games in a league or tournament
**Short pin**   a fallen pin that spins near a standing pin but fails to knock it over
**Sleeper**   a leave in which one pin is hidden directly behind another as in the 2-8, 3-9, or 1-5
**Slow lane**   a lane on which the ball hooks too much
**Sour apple**   a weak ball that leaves a 5-7, 5-10, or 5-7-10 split
**Span**   distance between the thumb and finger holes on a ball
**Spare**   all ten pins knocked down with two balls in a frame
**Split**   a leave in which the headpin is down and one or more spaces remain between or immediately in front of standing pins
**Spot bowling**   aiming at the arrows or other spots on the lane rather than at the pins
**Straight ball**   a ball rolled in a diagonal line toward the pocket
**Strike**   all ten pins knocked down with the first ball of a frame
**Strike out**   a strike in the last inning followed by two strikes on the bonus balls
**Sweeper**   a working ball that seems to sweep the pins into the pit

**Tap**   one pin left standing on an apparently perfect hit
**Telescore**   a device that projects the scoresheets on to a screen above the lanes
**Thin hit**   a ball hitting the side of a target pin causing considerable ball deflection
**Triple**   a turkey
**Turkey**   three strikes in a row

**Washout**   a 1-2-10 or 1-2-4-10 leave for right-handers or a 1-3-7 or 1-3-6-7 leave for left-handers
**WIBC**   Women's International Bowling Congress
**Woolworth**   a 5-10 split
**Working ball**   a ball that produces lots of pin action
**WPBA**   Women's Professional Bowlers Association

**YABA**   Young American Bowling Alliance; bowling organization for youth and college-age bowlers

# Appendix B
## *Bowling Resources*

### BOWLING ORGANIZATIONS

American Bowling Congress (ABC)
5301 South 76th Street
Greendale, WI 53129-0500

Women's International Bowling Congress (WIBC)
5301 South 76th Street
Greendale, WI 53129-0500

Young American Bowling Alliance (YABA)
5301 South 76th Street
Greendale, WI 53129-0500

Professional Bowlers Association (PBA)
P.O. Box 5118
1720 Merriman Road
Akron, Ohio 44313

Ladies Professional Bowlers Tour (LPBT)
(formerly the WPBA)
7171 Cherryvale Blvd.
Rockford, Illinois 61112

### MAGAZINES

*Bowling*, official publication of the ABC. See address above.

*The Woman Bowler*, official publication of the WIBC. See address above.

*Young American Bowling Alliance World*, official publication of the YABA. See address above.

*Bowlers Journal*, official publication of the Billiard and Bowling Institute of America, 200 Castlewood Dr., North Palm Beach, Florida 33408

# Appendix C
# *How Do You Stack Up?*

Answer the following questions. Then check your answers in Appendix D to see how well you have learned the concepts presented in this book. Review any information you did not understand. Your bowling scores will give you an indication of your physical skills.

## *TRUE-FALSE*

1. In the conventional grip, the fingers and thumb are inserted in the holes to the first joint.

2. The steps of the approach should increase in length from the first step through the slide or last step.

3. For the proper starting position in the four-step approach, most of the body weight is on the right foot to act as a reminder that the first step should be taken on the left foot.

4. A right-handed bowler begins the four-step approach on the right foot.

5. You should deliver the ball out over the foul line.

6. A medium-speed ball is often more effective than an extremely fast ball.

7. After the release, a bowler should lean away from the foul line and balance by stepping on the right foot.

8. In the four-step delivery, the ball is pushed away from the body on the second step.

9. The span is correct for a conventional grip if the knuckles reach about one-fourth inch beyond the nearest edge of the finger holes.

10. If two bowlers are ready to start their approaches, the bowler on the right is given the courtesy of bowling first.

11. You should pick up your ball with one hand.

12. The best strike pocket for a right-handed bowler is the 1-2 pocket.
13. Line bowling is a combination of pin bowling and spot bowling.
14. The position of the hand and wrist for the hook delivery is that of the normal handshake.
15. The curve ball delivery is better for beginners to learn.
16. The hand position for the straight ball before delivery is twelve o'clock for the thumb and six o'clock for the fingers.
17. A hook ball is better for creating strikes than a straight ball because there is more pin action.
18. The hook ball is easier to control than the straight ball.
19. A bowler with a great amount of hook should select a point of aim to the right of the second arrow for a strike ball.
20. The release point at the foul line for a strike should be in the vicinity of the center dot.
21. For leaves on the right side of the lane, the delivery should be made from the left.
22. The letters *ABC* refer to the national bowling organization called the American Bowling Congress.
23. In league bowling, members of a team bowl first on one lane and then on their opponent's lane.
24. The number 1 pin is called the kingpin.
25. A foul is charged against a player who steps over the foul detecting device to avoid fouling.
26. A strike in the tenth frame entitles the bowler to two more balls for a total of three balls.
27. It is possible to roll a score of 180 without ever making a strike.
28. Pitch refers to the degree of inclination the finger holes have toward the center of the ball.
29. Bowling is the top participant sport in the country.
30. A split occurs when a bowler's first ball hits too high on the headpin.

31. Your ability to pick up spares can make the difference between your becoming a low- or high-average bowler.

32. Lanes which have just been cleaned and oiled are usually fast and cut down the amount of hook on the ball.

33. In most situations after a split occurs, the average bowler should play it safe and attempt to get one pin of two, or two of three or four.

## *MULTIPLE-CHOICE*

Select the best answer for each statement.

34. The most commonly used approach is the:
    a. three-step approach
    b. four-step approach
    c. five-step approach
    d. none of these

35. The best bowling shoes are made of:
    a. a rubber sole for stopping and a leather sole for sliding
    b. two rubber soles for gripping the approach
    c. two leather soles to permit a shuffling-type step
    d. leather soles for sliding and rubber heels for stopping

36. Most professional bowlers:
    a. spot bowl the first ball and pin bowl the second ball
    b. use the spot aiming technique only with a straight ball
    c. use the pin technique of aiming because the pins are easier to see than the spot
    d. spot bowl both the first and second balls

37. Which of the following is a legal pinfall?
    a. pins rebounding from the side partition or rear cushion and downing pins
    b. pins knocked down by a ball that leaves the lane first
    c. ball rebounding from rear cushion and downing pins
    d. any part of the bowler's body crossing the foul line and touching the lane

38. If the pins are set incorrectly, but all ten are there, the bowler may:
    a. have the pins corrected before bowling
    b. accept the resulting pinfall

    c. replace the pins and rebowl
    d. both a and b

39. A scratch league is one in which:
    a. actual scores count
    b. a scratch figure is utilized and handicaps are figured and used
    c. bowlers are classified by ability
    d. only bowlers between certain set averages may enter

40. A bowler fouls on the first delivery of a frame. What is the proper procedure?
    a. pinfall counts; bowler forfeits second delivery
    b. pinfall does not count; bowler allowed second delivery
    c. pins are reset; bowler forfeits second delivery
    d. pins are reset; bowler forfeits first delivery

41. If Jane scored 180, 147, and 168 in three games, her average would be:
    a. 165
    b. 147
    c. 180
    d. 168

42. On a strike ball:
    a. the ball hits the 1, 3, 5, and 8 pins
    b. the ball hits the 1, 3, 5, and 9 pins
    c. the ball hits only the 1, 3, and 5 pins
    d. none of these

43. Fred, Mary, Tom, and Jane have averages of 60, 150, 190, and 145 respectively in a league that uses a scratch figure of 800 and 70 percent. Their team handicap, using the team method, is:
    a. 178
    b. 235
    c. 38
    d. 560

44. Fred's average is 60. His handicap in a league using 170 as a scratch score and 70 percent is:
    a. 42
    b. 60
    c. 77
    d. 119

45. When using marking to determine the winner, the total number of marks for this bowler would be:
   a. 7
   b. 8
   c. 9
   d. 10

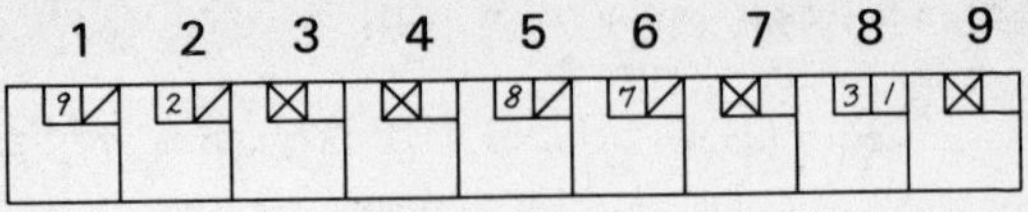

| 1 | 2 | 3 | 4 | 5 | 6 | 7 | 8 | 9 |
|---|---|---|---|---|---|---|---|---|
| 9 / | 2 / | X | X | 8 / | 7 / | X | 3 / | X |

## MATCHING

For each statement at the left, select the best answer or answers from the diagram at the right. Each answer may be used once, more than once, or not at all.

46. Straight ball

47. Backup ball

48. Hook ball

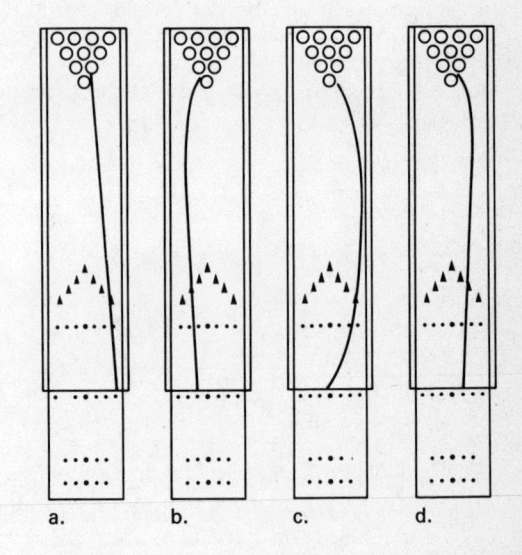

a.    b.    c.    d.

49. Split

50. No split

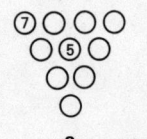

a. 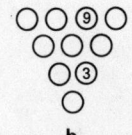    b. 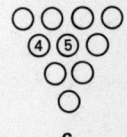    c.

d. 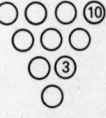    e.

110        BOWLING

# Bowling Crossword Puzzle

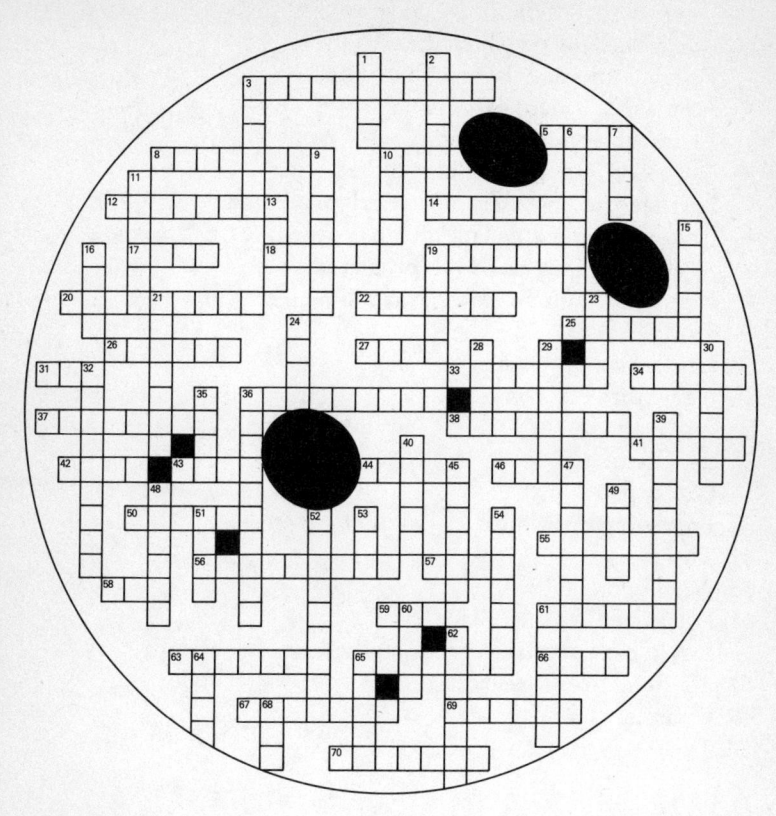

## ACROSS

3. 1-2-4-7 or 1-3-6-10
5. A lane on which the ball hooks too much
8. A split
10. Aiming at the arrows is called _____ bowling
12. A crossover
14. A slow lane
17. A frame without a mark is an _____ frame.
18. The number of points you earn in a game
19. Sum of game scores divided by number of games bowled
20. Brooklyn
22. Ball strikes pin at or near its center
25. Space between the 1 and 3 pins
26. All ten pins knocked down with one ball

*How Do You Stack Up?* 111

27. A 3-10 or 2-7 split is a _____ split.
31. One pin left standing after an apparently perfect hit
33. Part of the lane on which the pins stand
34. Ten pins knocked down with two balls
36. A lane that is hard to score on
37. An equalizer in competition
38. Ball rolled in a diagonal line to the pocket
41. Pins left standing after the first ball in a frame
42. Pins left lying on the lane after a delivery are _____ wood.
43. A slick lane that cuts down on ball hook
44. A score used for an absent player is a _____ score.
46. Blow; error
50. Last bowler on team
55. Game with 300 points
56. 7-10 split
57. miss; error
58. Object struck by ball
59. Professional bowling organization for men
61. Turkey
63. 2-8, 3-9, or 1-5 leave
65. A fast lane is a _____ lane.
66. Sweep bar used to clear pins off the lane after each delivery
67. 1-2-10 or 1-2-4-10 leave
69. Channel
70. 1 pin

## DOWN

1. An effective ball that doesn't "work" is a _____ ball.
2. 4-6-7-10 split
3. Knocking down the front pin of a leave and leaving the rear pin
6. Organized groups of teams competing on a regular basis
7. Women's bowling organization
9. A bucket
10. Distance between thumb and finger holes on a ball
11. Spots on the lane at which a bowler aims
13. A ball that hits the headpin straight on is a _____ hit.
15. A leave in which the headpin is down and spaces remain between or in front of standing pins
16. A strike or spare
19. A lane
21. A league using actual scores is a _____ league.

23. A ball that breaks sharply toward the center during its last few feet nearest the pins.
24. Youth bowling organization
28. An upward motion of the ball given by the fingers at release
29. Three games
30. A very shallow depression on a lane; ball track
32. Machine that resets the pins
35. Women's professional bowling organization
36. A ball rolled in the channel
39. Projects scores on screen above lanes
40. Angle of holes drilled in ball
45. Two consecutive strikes
47. Working ball that sweeps pins into the pit
48. A frame
49. Ball lands some distance from the foul line due to a late release
51. Ball hitting on headpin side of 1-3 pocket
52. 5-10 split
53. Depression behind pin deck into which pins fall
54. Game of tenpins
60. Object rolled at pins in bowling
61. Three strikes in a row
62. 5 pin
64. A game
65. A ball provided by a bowling center is a _____ ball.
68. Bowling organization for men

# Appendix D
# Answers to Problems and Questions

## CHAPTER 2

**Scoring** (page 50)

| Name | 1 | 2 | 3 | 4 | 5 | 6 | 7 | 8 | 9 | 10 | Total |
|---|---|---|---|---|---|---|---|---|---|---|---|
| Heidi | 9 | 29 | 49 | 68 | 77 | 91 | 109 | 117 | 145 | 165 | 165 |
| Chris | 9 | 39 | 65 | 83 | 91 | 114 | 134 | 144 | 150 | 176 | 176 |

## CHAPTER 4

**Averages** (page 75)

1. Diego's average is 156

2. Lorna's average is 151

3. Their team average is 648

**Handicaps** (page 77)

1. Alana's handicap is 18 (180−159=21×.9=18)

2. Bob's handicap is 13 (200−183=17×.8=13)

3. Their team handicap is 108
   | | | | | | |
   |---|---|---|---|---|---|
   | Doug | 200 | 159 | 41 | .7 | 28.7 |
   | Geniece | 200 | 165 | 35 | .7 | 24.5 |
   | Larry | 200 | 183 | 17 | .7 | 11.9 |
   | Mossi | 200 | 135 | 65 | .7 | 45.5 |
   | | | | | | 108 |

4. Their team handicap is 129
   | | | | | | |
   |---|---|---|---|---|---|
   | Valais | 200 | 165 | 35 | .8 | 28 |
   | Loni | 200 | 141 | 59 | .8 | 47.2 |
   | Ben | 200 | 156 | 44 | .8 | 35.2 |
   | Charles | 200 | 176 | 24 | .8 | 19.2 |
   | | | | | | 129 |

5. Their team handicap is 135
   135 + 158 + 143 + 183 = 619
   800 − 619 = 181 × .75 = 135.75

6. Their team handicap is 156
   176 + 141 + 163 + 146 = 626
   800 − 626 = 174 × .9 = 156.6

**Marking** (page 84)

| Name | 1 | 2 | 3 | 4 | 5 | 6 | 7 | 8 | 9 | 10 | Total Hcp 63 |
|---|---|---|---|---|---|---|---|---|---|---|---|
| Than (27) | 6 / 12 | 2 / 32 | X 52 | 5 / 70 | 8 1 / 79 | X 103 | X 123 | 4 / 143 | X 156 | F 3 159 | 222 |
| Maria (36) | F / 12 | 2 / 32 | X 57 | X 77 | 5 / 87 | 6 9 96 | 8 / 116 | X 129 | 2 1 132 | 3 / 4 146 | 368 |
| marks (6) | ½ 8 | 2½ 8 | ½ 10 | ⅓ 13 | 1 14 | 1 1 14 | ⅓ 17 | 1½ 18 | 1 1 18 | | |

| Name | 1 | 2 | 3 | 4 | 5 | 6 | 7 | 8 | 9 | 10 | Total Hcp 49 |
|---|---|---|---|---|---|---|---|---|---|---|---|
| Denise (18) | X 14 | 2 2 18 | 6 / 38 | X 58 | 6 / 73 | 5 / 83 | F 9 92 | X 116 | X 136 | 4 / 156 | 205 |
| Ron (31) | X 14 | 3 1 18 | X 44 | X 64 | 6 / 84 | X 104 | 9 / 116 | 2 / 126 | F 8 134 | 3 4 141 | 346 |
| marks (5) | ½ 7 | ½ 5 | ½ 7 | ⅓ 10 | 1½ 12 | ½ 14 | 1 1 14 | 1½ 15 | 1½ 16 | | |

## APPENDIX C (pages 106–110)

| | | | | |
|---|---|---|---|---|
| 1. F | 11. F | 21. T | 31. T | 41. a |
| 2. T | 12. F | 22. T | 32. T | 42. b |
| 3. F | 13. T | 23. T | 33. F | 43. a |
| 4. T | 14. T | 24. F | 34. b | 44. c |
| 5. T | 15. F | 25. T | 35. a | 45. a |
| 6. T | 16. T | 26. T | 36. d | 46. a |
| 7. F | 17. T | 27. T | 37. a | 47. b |
| 8. F | 18. F | 28. T | 38. d | 48. d |
| 9. T | 19. T | 29. T | 39. a | 49. a, c, e |
| 10. T | 20. F | 30. T | 40. d | 50. b, d |

*Answers to Problems and Questions*

## CROSSWORD PUZZLE ANSWER

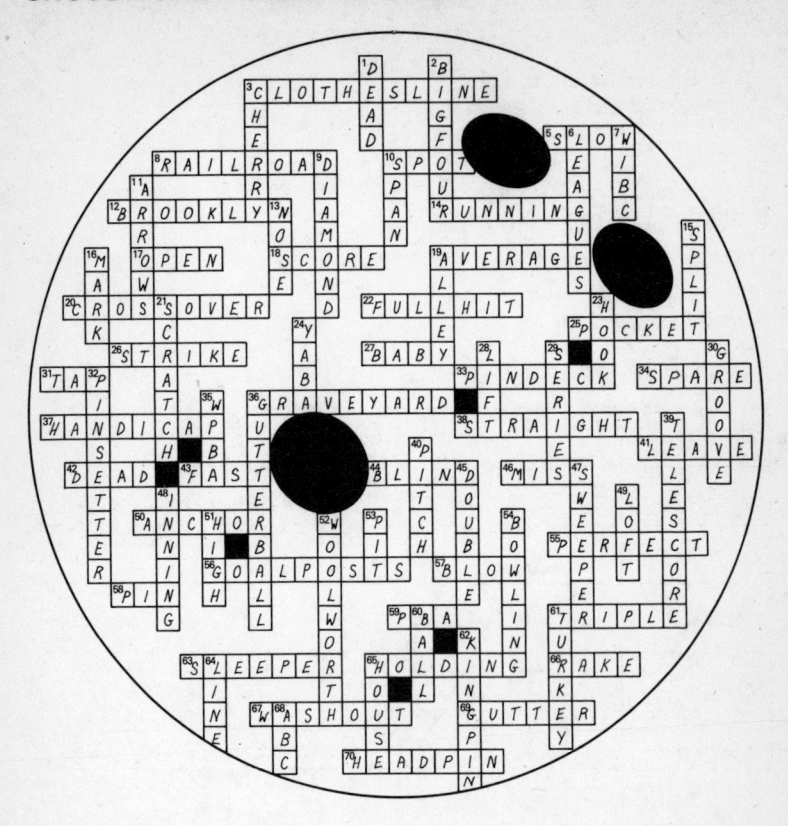

# Appendix E
# Challenge Activities

## OBJECTIVE

The completion of any or all of the challenge activities will increase your overall knowledge and enjoyment of the game of bowling.

1. **TV Match:**  Watch a professional bowlers' TV match. Include an analysis of each bowler (number of steps, type of ball, speed of approach, etc.) and your analysis of the match.

2. **League Bowling:**  Watch a team bowling match at a commercial lane. Report on one team including name and average of each bowler followed by an analysis of his or her style (number of steps, type of ball, etc.)

3. **Bowling in a League:**  Bowl as a member of a team at school or at a commercial lane. Report your participation with proof of games bowled.

4. **Analysis of Another Bowler:**  Use "Analyzing Your Game—Common Faults and Remedies" to assist another bowler to improve his or her game. Report in chart form faults, suggested corrections, and results, along with the amount of time spent in helping the bowler.

## Analyzing Your Game—Common Faults and Remedies
## OBJECTIVE

Upon completion of this activity you will be aware of your performance, know your problem areas, and be able to correct them to build consistency in your game.

**Written Assignment:**  Read the section on bowling analysis in Chapter 2 of this text or in other bowling texts. Complete the following:

1. Poor timing, resulting in poor balance, being "ahead of the ball," etc., can be corrected by _____

2. Drifting (failure to walk in a straight line) can be corrected by _____

3. Too low or no backswing, resulting in insufficient ball speed, can be corrected by _____

4. "Lofting" the ball may be caused by _____

5. A "hop" in the approach can be corrected by _____

6. "Side-wheeling" is another term for _____

**Skill Assignment:** Use the following analysis chart to analyze your bowling. (It's best to have another bowler analyze you; however, you can analyze yourself.)

1. Make sure you are committing the fault frequently.
2. After you have determined the problem, try one adjustment at a time according to the suggestions you have read.
3. Be sure you continue doing other phases of your game as you were prior to changing the fault.
4. Practice your corrections slowly at first. It's better to practice *without* keeping score until you feel the fault has been corrected.

**Analysis Chart:** Place a check (✓) on the line *each* time the fault is evident.

**The Approach:** Circle the number of steps    3    4    5

1. Timing problems _____
   (symptoms—ahead of the ball, hop or hesitation in approach, charging the line, forcing the swing)

2. Drifting _____
   (crooked walk to foul line)

## *The Delivery:*

1. Shoulders not square to foul line _____
   (parallel to line)

2. Forcing the forward swing _____
   (symptoms—throwing the ball, dropping the ball)

3. Lofting _____
   ("throwing" the ball several feet beyond the foul line)

4. Carrying the ball _____
   (hesitation in swing; not getting the ball away on the first step)

5. Crooked swing _____
   (ball brought behind body in backswing; out from body in back or forward swing)

6. Wrist or arm twisting _____
   (twist of wrist/arm during backswing, forward swing, or release)

7. High backswing _____
   (symptoms—hips or shoulders turn, delay at top of backswing)

8. Loss of balance at delivery _____
   (unable to hold finishing position at foul line)

9. Hop in delivery _____

10. Side-wheeling _____
    (wide pendulum swing)

## *Ball Release:*

1. Not enough/too much finger lift _____
   (ball too straight or too much curve/hook)

2. Poor or no follow-through _____
   ("dumping" ball; bouncing ball)

3. Flipping the ball _____
   (ball too straight; some lofting)

4. Pulling the ball _____
   (high hit; follow-through across body)

5. Foot turned at foul line _____
   (missed target arrow; balance loss)

6. Taking eyes off target _____
   (pull ball; poor balance; no follow-through)

## *Ball Roll:*

1. Ball too fast _____
   (pins fly, no movement, speed from foul line to pins less than 2-1/4 seconds = too fast)

2. Ball too slow _____
   (pins fall slowly, speed from foul line to pins more than 3 seconds = too slow)

3. "Killing the hook" _____
   (not getting hook ball)

4. Too much hook/curve _____
   (ball too light; ball speed too slow)

5. High hit _____
   (full headpin hit; cherry; missed arrow)

6. Light hit _____
   (not getting up to pin; missed arrow)

7. Missed target (arrow) _____

Record your fault(s) and the correction(s) for each, along with the date you began practice for correction and the date you felt correction was successful. Then, contact your instructor to watch you.

| Fault | Correction | Date started | Date successful |
|---|---|---|---|
| Example: Drifting | Practiced walking along the board | March 3 | March 10 |
|  |  |  |  |

Challenge Activities

# Index

Absentee score, 76
Address, 20, 24–27
Adjusting to lane conditions, 87–89
Advanced bowling strategies, 66, 85
Aiming, 51–56
   Line bowling, 53, 56
   Pin bowling, 52
   Spot bowling, 52–55
   Strike, 51–52, 59–61
American Bowling Congress, 12, 105
Angle adjustments, 58–70
   2-4-6, 61, 65–66, 67
   3-6-9, 61, 64–65, 67
   7-pin shot, 60–61, 64, 66
   10-pin shot, 60–61, 64, 66
   Spares, 60–70
   Strikes, 59–61
Answers to problems and questions, 114–116
Approach, 4, 5
   Four-step approach. *See* Four-step approach
   One-step approach, 16–19
Armswing, 20–21, 25
Arrows on lane, 4–5
Averages, 73–74, 77

Backswing, 21, 31–33, 34
Backup ball, 53, 56–57
Ball, 4–8, 90
Ball, drilling, 6–8, 41, 90–91
Ball, fit, 7
Ball, picking up safely, 16, 23
Ball return, 4–5
Ball return rack, 4

Ball roll patterns, 53–58
   Backup ball, 53, 56–57
   Curve ball, 53, 57–58
   Hook ball, 53, 57–58
   Straight ball, 53, 56–57, 58
Ball speed, 41
Benefits of bowling, 13
Blind bowlers, 13
Boards on lanes, 4, 58–59
Body English, 15
Bowling center, 2–4
Bowling magazines, 105
Bowling organizations, 105

Challenge activities, 117–121
Channels, 5
Compensation, 96–97
Competitive bowling, 71–72
Conditioning, 9–10, 17
Confidence, 93–96
Crossword puzzle, 111–113
   Answer to crossword puzzle, 116
Curve ball, 53, 57–58

Dead wood, 4
Dictionary, 101–104
Downswing, 20, 31–32
Dress, 1–2

Equipment, 2–9
Equipment changes, advanced, 89–91
Error Corrector
   Backswing, 34

Ball errors, 40
Footwork, 26
Forward swing, 35
Pushaway, 29
Release, 38
Stance, 27
Etiquette, 14-15
Exercises, conditioning, 9-10, 17

Feedback, 39
Five-step approach, 36, 39
Follow-through, 21, 36, 39
Footwork, 20-23, 26
Forward swing, 21, 33-35
Foul, 45-48
Foul lights, 4
Foul line, 4-5
Four-step approach, 16, 19-39
  Address or stance, 20, 23-27
  Armswing, 20-21, 25
  Backswing, 21, 31-33, 34
  Downswing, 20, 31-32
  Follow-through, 21, 36, 39
  Footwork, 20-23, 26
  Forward swing, 21, 33-35
  Pushaway, 20, 25-31
  Release, 21, 34-38
  Shake-hands grip, 18, 24, 37, 58
  Timing, 36
Frame, 6, 14, 44-50
Fun games and tournaments, 68-70, 80-81

Game, 14
Game, perfect, 14
Grips, 6-7
Grip, shake-hands, 18, 24, 37, 58
Gutter, 5

Handicaps, 74-77
  Individual, 74
  Team, 74-76
History, 10-13
Hook ball, 53, 57-58
House ball, 6

Kickbacks, 3, 5

Lane, 3-5
Lane conditions, 85-89
Lane construction, 4, 5
Leagues, 72-79
  Rules, 76-79
  Types, 72
Left-handed bowling, 17, 19
Line, 14
Line bowling, 53

Marking, 81-84
Martin Luther, 12
Mental aspects, 92-97

Ninepins, 13

One-step approach, 16-19

Pacer, 78
Perfect game, 14
Picking up ball, 16, 23
Pin bowling, 52
Pin deck, 3, 87
Pinfall, 48-49
  Dead ball, 49
  Illegal, 48
  Legal, 48
Pins, 3
  Headpin, 3
  Kingpin, 3
  Set-up, 3
Pinsetters, 3-4
Pit, 4-5
Pitch, 6-8
Pocket, 51
Practice schedule, 39, 99
Pushaway, 20, 25-31

Rake, 4
Rangefinder, 4-5

Reading the lanes, 85–87
Rear cushion, 4–5
Release, 21, 34–38
Reset button, 4
Resources, 105

Safety, 15–16
Scoring, 6, 44–51
   Double, 46–47
   Error, miss, blow, 46
   Fouls, 45–48
   Gutter ball, 45–46
   Mark, 45
   Open frame, 44–45
   Perfect game, 14
   Spare, 6, 14, 44, 46. *See also* Aiming and Angle adjustments
   Split, 46–48
   Strike, 6, 14, 44–46. *See also* Aiming and Angle adjustments
   Strike out, 46
   Tenth frame, 45, 49
   Turkey, triple, 46
Series, 78
Seven-pin position for aiming, 60–61, 64, 66
Shake-hands grip, 18, 24, 37, 58
Shoes, 2
Sir Flinders Petrie, 10
Sir Francis Drake, 12
Span, 6
Spare. *See* Scoring
Sport experience
   Aiming, 54
   Angle adjustments
      Spares, 67–70
      Strikes, 62–63
   Averages, 75
   Backswing, 33
   Ball, 90
   Ball selection, 7, 41
   Bowling center, 6
   Confidence, 94–95
   Downswing, 32
   Etiquette, 17
   Follow-through, 39
   Footwork, 23
   Forward swing, 35
   Four-step approach, 20, 42
   Handicaps, 77
   Lane conditions, 87
      Adjustments to, 89
   League play, 80
   Marking, 84
   One-step approach, 19
   Pushaway, 28
   Release, 37
   Safety, 18
   Scoring, 50
   Stance, 25
   Strikes, 60
   Warm-ups, 10
Sport for Life, 1, 100
Spot bowling, 52–53
Stance, 20, 23–27
Straight ball, 53, 56–58
Strategies, advanced, 66, 85
Strike. *See* Scoring
Strike ball action, 51–52

Telescore, 2–3
Ten-pin position for aiming, 60–61, 64, 66
Test, 106–110
Three-six-nine method of aiming, 61, 64–65, 67
Three-step approach, 36, 39
Timing, 36
Tournaments, 79–81
Trouble button, 4
Two-four-six method of aiming, 61, 65–67

Videotape replay, 41

Warm-ups, 9–10, 17
Women's International Bowling Congress, 12, 105